A Woman's Guide
to the
World of Sailing

A Woman's Guide to the World of Sailing

The Dreams and Realities of Cruising, Crossing, and Competitive Racing

by

Jane Golden

SEAWORTHY PUBLICATIONS, INC.　●　MELBOURNE, FLORIDA

A Woman's Guide to the World of Sailing
The Dreams and Realities of Cruising, Crossing, and Competitive Racing
Copyright ©2023 by Jane Golden

Published in the USA by:
Seaworthy Publications, Inc.
6300 N Wickham Rd.
Unit #130-416
Melbourne, FL 32940
Phone 321-389-2506
e-mail orders@seaworthy.com
www.seaworthy.com

Library of Congress Cataloging-in-Publication Data

Names: Golden, Jane, 1955- author.
Title: A woman's guide to the world of sailing : the dreams and realities
 of cruising, crossing, and competitive racing / by Jane Golden.
Description: Melbourne, Florida : Seaworthy Publications, Inc., [2023] |
 Summary: "Jane Golden has been a sailor for most of her life, beginning
 with some raucous experiences as a young adult volunteer crew member on
 other people's sailboats. Fast forward and she was cruising the Gulf
 Coast with family and friends on her own boat, Gypsy Lady. After an
 enjoyable description of her Gulf Coast experiences, Jane ventures to
 Europe where she first charter sailed with friends, and later crossed
 the Atlantic Ocean as a crewmember for the Atlantic Rally for Cruisers.
 She goes into great depth about the positives and negatives of such
 events; including how they are organized, the peculiarities and politics
 of such events, and what it was like to be a part of the crew on a
 transatlantic crossing. Finally, she writes about the very enjoyable
 experiences supporting Gypsy Lady and her family's participation in the
 annual Regata al Sol from Pensacola to Mexico, a regional yacht club
 race that began in the early 60's. The descriptions of the Regata al Sol
 event founder, and the post-race celebrations, are a treasure trove of
 details that would make anyone want to participate in the race and the
 festivities. Jane gives us a compelling look at her experiences as a
 woman in the world of sailing, and great descriptions of the various
 kinds of sailing, racing, and cruising in which she has participated.
 Her book informs, instructs, and entertains"-- Provided by publisher.
Identifiers: LCCN 2023028018 (print) | LCCN 2023028019 (ebook) | ISBN
 9781948494793 (paperback) | ISBN 9781948494809 (epub)
Subjects: LCSH: Women sailors--United States--Biography. | Sailors--United
 States--Biography. | Women travelers--United States--Biography. |
 Sailing for women. | Yacht racing.
Classification: LCC GV810.92.G65 A3 2023 (print) | LCC GV810.92.G65
 (ebook) | DDC 797.124082--dc23/eng/20230726
LC record available at https://lccn.loc.gov/2023028018
LC ebook record available at https://lccn.loc.gov/2023028019

Dedication

To Jordana, Greer, and Pippa:
future sailors of the world.

Prologue

I t would all be fine. What I needed was for the race to get started.

The fireworks announcing our impending departure ended at ten the following evening, but unlike past regattas I've attended where crews were already wasted and parties just beginning, the enormous marina was eerily quiet. Most of the last-minute details were completed for our boat. Perhaps other tasks were destined to be left undone, only to weigh on the minds of captains and crew. Maybe the quiet was due to concern over the anticipated poor weather for the start. Whatever it was, the usual sense of revelry wasn't there—perhaps the winds had consumed it.

Winds were already blowing at the predicted 26 knots and gusting over 35 in the early morning. Flags and pennants were plastered across the sky. Everyone knew that the exit of 76 large sailboats from the marina in the man-made harbor would be crowded, notwithstanding a slightly staggered start. Waves were predicted to be over ten feet once outside the jetties, even if the wind moderated to a perfect 20 knots. I voted to wait a day for better weather, but it wasn't a democracy and no one even took notice of my vote. The regatta would start on the day it was planned, with parties in Cape Verde set in stone—weather be damned and full speed ahead.

"If a man must be obsessed by something,
I suppose a boat is as good as anything,
perhaps a bit better than most. A small
sailing craft is not only beautiful, it is
seductive and full of strange promise and
the hint of trouble."

E. B. White

Part One
Destin to Key West &
Biloxi to Carabelle

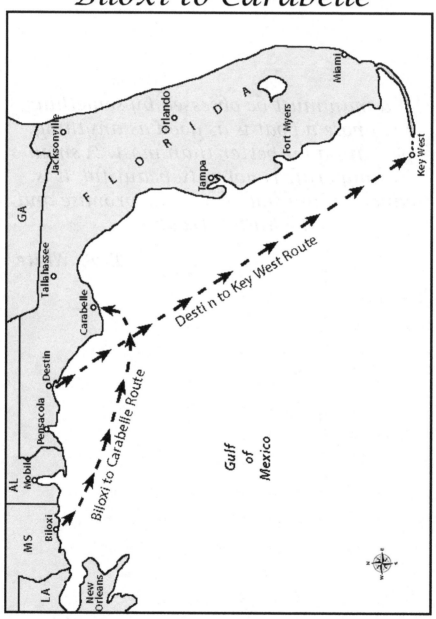

Chapter One

*T*he Commodores released the song "Sail On" in the summer of 1979. That was the same year I became a sailor.

It began innocently enough, with road trips in my Mercury Cougar with a group of fellow students to northwest Florida, otherwise known as the Panhandle, to sail in weekend races at the Fort Walton Beach Yacht Club, where a friend of a friend had a small Cheoy Lee sailboat. It was the ultimate come on, each sailing experience better than the one before— the winds were compliant, the sun bright, and the beer free. Soon I had a good grasp on the fundamentals of sailing, plus a "great" tan to go with my bleached blonde hair. A few weeks later, not only were we winning races, but I knew enough to pass as an acceptable weekender at the yacht club, both on a boat and in the evening around the sprawling piers and grounds.

We outsiders created such a buzz in the otherwise calm club, that it wasn't long until our friend's mother's ex-husband became keenly interested in our group. He needed some crew to sail a 54-foot trimaran to Key West, and we were the right people to accompany him in this endeavor during the height of hurricane season. He no doubt found us to be the perfect crew: full of bravado, young and naïve. I had heard stories about him—that maybe he had been a foreign mercenary, but the stories were so outlandish, that I thought none of them could be true. Who actually did that?

The captain/supposed owner of the trimaran was about age sixty, weathered, and full of stories of far-away places and the people he had met. He looked like Spencer Tracey after a hard week of drinking and was in the middle of one of his many divorces, hence his sudden need to take the boat to the Keys. It only took an hour in a Fort Walton dive bar for him to buy enough beers to convince my roommate, me, and two guys from school to sign on as his unpaid crew from Destin to Key West.

It sounded like a great idea to me—it was summer break, and the boat was beautiful. Only one of the two guys offered a good reason for going. He had previously sailed a trimaran up the East Coast and given the lack of an otherwise seasoned crew, he figured that we would all die if he wasn't there in case of an emergency.

In addition to the five of us there was a perpetually sea-sick boat mechanic. The captain hired him to keep the malfunctioning engine operational. In retrospect, it was a bad sign, one I had missed, that we needed a full-time mechanic. He was a tall, skinny, quiet country boy from rural Alabama, his skin as white as a sheet. Each time the engine failed, which was most of the time, he'd go below and then promptly get seasick. It didn't take long for him to become miserable.

In hindsight I should have told him on that first day to leave the boat and go home. I didn't tell him that it was a dumb idea to take a trip on the open Gulf in the middle of hurricane season, especially if you get seasick and sunburnt. I probably should have also told him to get paid in advance.

All the signs that things may not be right were there within hours of our departure, beginning with nagging questions about ownership of the sailboat. While we students were ordering rum drinks at the bar (on the captain's credit card, of course), several IRS agents showed up at the dock looking for him—and it should have made us wonder why he was suddenly unable to be found. Other signs appeared soon after, such as the boat's lack of any working navigational system, and the rumors of ships our captain had lost off the coast of Cuba. The evidence that he was completely crazy took longer to appear.

All the same, it was easy to ignore any bad omens on the spectacular summer morning when we cast off the dock lines and headed due south. Destin back then was a sleepy fishing town around a large natural harbor with emerald-green waters and pristine white shores. In the '70s there were no towering condominiums or jet skis swarming the harbor entrance like buzzing mosquitoes; it was still a town meant for those who wanted to get up at dawn and head out to fish. Small bait shops and chandleries once sat where the latest version of a Crabby Joes or four-story souvenir shops now sell food and wares to the hundreds of thousands of tourists. The quiet is gone now, but the beaches remain the same—some of the most beautiful in the world.

On that morning in 1979 we left with calm seas, a gentle wind in our sails, and not a cloud on the horizon. For endless hours we moved past one point on the chart to another with little to do other than adjust a sail here or there. Mostly, we lazed about, pleased with ourselves for snagging the trip.

The first days of the sail were a lot like summer camp in junior high, when children divide up into cliques. When they were talking at all, the captain and the mechanic would go below and discuss the engine, which I assumed that he was fixing in order to sell the boat. My roommate had cornered the guy she liked and spent her days with him. That left the blond-haired guy who happened to be from Florida, stuck teaching me the more nuanced points of sailing that you don't learn on an afternoon race.

Then one afternoon, for no known reason, the captain shattered the trip's peaceful façade. He angrily emerged from below with his old hat on, looking like a throw-back from a 1940s movie, watery blue eyes squinting in the sun, and summoned us around him. Then he opened a large locker exposing an arsenal of weapons.

"If anyone tries to board, we shoot to kill— do you understand that?" Our four startled heads bobbed up and down as he stared into our eyes.

"Do you know how to shoot weapons?" He asked each of us, one at a time. I said yes, but of course I was lying— I'd never even seen those types of firearms. Apparently satisfied, the captain retreated below to do whatever he did down there.

After this incident, the captain seemed to grow increasingly crazier as the trip's windless days progressed. Soon I became his target for verbal abuse. From the time that I refused to change course in order to use a sea turtle for target practice (he was bored) to blaming me for the malfunctioning compass—it had to be my nearby stash of canned goods causing the problem—I was fast approaching the status of first person overboard.

Making the tension even worse, the further south we sailed, the more unpredictable the weather became. Amidst lighter winds overall, August lightning storms began to pop up around us, the thunder often sounding like rapid gunfire. The hatch above my berth leaked and my mattress was consistently wet.

We outran or simply avoided most really bad storms, except for one night when the black clouds came up so quickly that we had only time to drop and secure the mainsail. Our boat was forced off-course when the smaller mizzen sail at the back of the boat, ripped and wrapped around its spreader. No amount of tugging would pull it down. It was then that I learned that a trimaran or catamaran can "pitch-pole."

This phenomenon occurs when the wind gets behind and under the boat and throws its stern over the bow like a somersault. I was matter-of-factly informed that if this occurred, I would likely die. Of course, I only received this information in the screaming moments when a lightning bolt lit the night and we scrambled to contain the mizzen as the boat flew over the tops of the waves and burrowed into their troughs. Mother nature, for the moment, clearly had the upper hand.

It was then that the guy instructing me, the only one with experience on a trimaran, wisely took over the helm, barking orders that we should try and relieve the pressure the wind was exerting on the boat. When he saw me clinging to a lifeline as the boat slammed over the waves, he yelled to the others:

"Get a life preserver on her – NOW!"

All the while, the useless captain was below calling the Coast Guard and yelling Mayday. Occasionally I would hear a young Coast Guard officer say, "Take down your sails captain," and, "What is your location captain?" That last one was funny, since the captain didn't know where we were. Eventually, we lost radio contact altogether.

For hours the boat maintained its forward momentum, continuing to surf forward at the same speed as the storm, hurling us to some unknown destination. At times the pontoons would dig into a wave and the wind would lift the stern high enough to make us hold our breath and pray.

And then… just as always happens, the storm played out and the seas began to calm. It seemed that we would survive after all—but where were we? Given the wind's direction and our lack of navigation, it could have been Cuba.

Our joy at seeing two fishing boats six hours later was short-lived. The sailors only spoke Spanish and didn't seem inclined to help a boat like us: ripped sails, exhausted sailors, and a stupid captain. We probably looked like drug runners. Pointing us toward Key West was the only help they could afford.

Before the advent of the GPS and lacking a functioning Loran C or even a sextant, our only option was to hold up a battery-operated transistor radio for directional signals. Our course was literally dictated by a small black radio playing the Eric Clapton song Cocaine over and over again. If we sailed toward the direction of the signal and it got louder, then we assumed that we were headed to the radio station on Key West. I still hate that song.

By then we also didn't have enough food, and as the cook I was the culprit for that as well—even though I wasn't the one who provisioned. My roommate and her guy-friend began to look at me like I was the outsider in a bizarre horror movie.

It's no wonder that when our dock lines eventually hit the harbor pier on Stock Island (near Key West), I did what so many others who have been at sea for a while do. At the first opportunity I jumped from the boat to the dock on wobbly sea legs and landed right in the water, surrounded by jelly fish, seaweed, and smelly diesel. There was no pity to spare for me, however; even with a banged foot I was expected to help clean the boat while the captain left to check on the potential sale.

Late that afternoon, a well-fed and intoxicated captain returned and gave us the evening "off." Of course, town was miles away, and I had less than five dollars. My roommate used her father's credit card meant for school expenses to rent a hotel room and order room service for her and her increasingly close friend. I had no credit card.

Without other options, the blond sailor and I decided that we had to get away from the boat and find some space to think about our situation. Our best option was to hitch-hike to Key West for dinner.

We mistakenly jumped into the car of a guy who announced he had to make a "business" stop at a trailer along the way.

"Hey man, that's okay with you right?"

Of course, it wasn't okay in the least, but we were stuck and sat quietly in the back seat of his car. After a maze of turns, he stopped to make his deal at a run-down trailer at the end of a long sandy road through mangrove trees. I might not have recognized how dangerous the sailboat trip was, but I knew a drug deal when I saw one and I wanted to be anywhere but where I was at that moment.

As soon as we reached a paved road, we asked to be dropped off at the first possible restaurant. This was before the days of cute pink restaurants and shops on every corner; at the time, most Key West homes were just ordinary shacks where people slept at night and left to go fishing in the daytime. It was still an outpost town, filled with people who wanted to escape the "normal," and its charm was as a raw, salty outpost. Battered by storms and far from big stores and easy travel, it was an Ernest Hemingway kind of place—or at least the side of it that we saw that night.

Before I could take a bite out of my Cuban sandwich, which was paid for with the last of my money and had just been placed before me on the worn Formica tabletop, I heard the deafening sirens of a speeding police car. I ducked in fear as it jumped the curb outside my window and headed towards a man who must have been stabbed and was lying in a pool of blood on the nearby sidewalk.

I knew then that it was time for my Key West adventure to end.

"I want to go home," I said with a sigh as I watched the scene unfold.

The next morning the sailor friend and I secretly packed our meager belongings and went to town. Moe, the kind barber on Duval Street, cashed a $40.00 check for us and we took the first bus out of town. I guess some might think us criminals for jumping ship, but we were more like trafficking victims managing an escape.

I still remember everything about the bus ride late that afternoon. As I sat safely on the vinyl Greyhound bus seat speeding north over the many bridges linking the Keys to the rest of the state, I soaked in the beauty of the mangroves, bougainvillea, and palm trees. I snapped mental pictures of the turquoise waters.

Soon I would reach the home of a friend in Coral Gables, but as the sun set over the horizon, washing the sky in bright orange, I nestled my head into my friend's shoulder and smiled in contentment. I had sailed across the Gulf of Mexico and seen Key West. Life was good.

Chapter Two

*T*he big question came in a such a sailorly way. Over the next year my friend from Key West became a whole lot more—a person with a name—Jay. He was everything I dreamed about: a true blond-haired surfer boy, and smart. He liked the fact that I never complained on the Key West trip, and I liked the fact that he made me laugh. Having both grown up on beaches—he surfing the Atlantic and I fishing in the Gulf— it was only natural that we would be compatible, but I never imagined anything more long-term. I thought we would one day graduate from law school and go our separate ways, to our own separate waters. Sailing had been a short-term thrill.

Then unexpectedly everything changed. I'll never forget the exact spot where that happened.

It was a spring morning in Birmingham, with mountains of azaleas in bloom and the future as bright as the sun. Jay and I had enjoyed a good Southern breakfast and were driving my car through Mountainbrook's maze of curving roads, admiring the expansive neighborhood full of stately homes. We had not a penny or worry in the world.

Right as we exited the neighborhood and encountered the ugly interstate intersection near the mall, Jay fell quiet for a few seconds, took a deep breath, and intently looked straight ahead with both hands on the wheel, avoiding my face. It was like he was staring down an enemy army headed his way. Several seconds passed before he summoned his courage to speak.

"I want you to know that I don't have any intention of getting married."

I was quiet. Where did this come from? Poor thing. Had he held this thought in all weekend, wondering when to tell me?

He continued with a more confident voice when I didn't begin to weep and wail.

"My plan is to not get married, and when I'm sixty I'll buy a sailboat and then I'll get a younger girl to go with me and keep me company. That's always been my plan… I just thought you ought to know so you don't think anything…" He still didn't look my way.

I returned the seriousness with which he spoke, also looking straight ahead. I told him I didn't know why he ever thought I wanted to marry him. I told him that his plan sounded great. He relaxed, I relaxed, and we didn't talk about it again.

He and I didn't talk about it, but I did go home and tell my mother that it looked like I was getting married. All smart girls know that once the word "marriage" slips across a lover's lips, it's only a matter of time until it occurs. The trick is to play it right—and I did.

He was already hooked, and that day was his last gasp to spit the hook. If I had made a scene, he would have expelled me from his life like the whale coughed up Jonah, with little effort. He would go with some of his mates to the nearest bar and put down a few beers, happy to be free and on the loose again. Unfortunately for Jay, I grew up in a home full of brothers and knew how to play the game better than he did.

As I predicted, only a matter of months passed before we were engaged, never to discuss the "sailboat at sixty" plan again. My apologies to any woman he intended to invite onto his sailboat later in life.

We were married during the height of inflation, when interest rates on a home were 15% and you could only secure a mortgage if you already had lots of money. We didn't have lots of money. And when you can't afford to go out to eat or take fancy vacations or landscape your estate, you stay home and have babies. Without insurance or paid leave, we did just that—had one after the other, only stopping at three in three years.

Jennie was first, then Harrison, and lastly Patrick. All three are as different as can be, yet connected to each other in wonderful ways. I attribute much of that to the *Lotus*.

Totally dependent upon extremely favorable owner financing from our friend, the *Lotus* came into our lives at about the same time the last of my three children began to walk. The children were also financed, but by an unfriendly hospital with interest.

Our *Lotus* was the 27-foot Cheoy Lee that had won those Fort Walton races all those years ago, the first boat that I had learned to sail on. It had everything our small family needed: a tiny sink, a head, and a tiller to die for. With a one-cylinder Volvo diesel engine that sounded and moved like the African Queen, it took us everywhere in the northern Gulf, even when the weather was against us.

We spent our spring breaks sleeping on the boat at the stately Grand Hotel marina in Fairhope, at a cost of $1.00 a foot per night. The children swam, fished, played putt-putt, and rode bicycles among the moss-laden oak trees and ponds full of ducks, just the same as if they were in an expensive hotel room—all for $27.00 a day. Our menu consisted of pop-tarts and milk in the morning, peanut butter sandwiches and chips for lunch, and barbeque sandwiches from Ben's for supper: – unhealthy, but universally appreciated.

My vacation treat on each trip was one meal in the elegant Grand Hotel restaurant, where the children would dress up in the matching outfits I made for them, and I'd have a glass of wine and we'd look every bit like we belonged there.

There was nothing more that we could need on spring breaks and summer vacations than the *Lotus*, our safe and sturdy bucket. Years after we sold the *Lotus*, I asked my father why in the world he let us take his grandchildren out in the Gulf in bad weather (we were always time-constrained and sailed on the calendar, not necessarily the weather window). He said that he trusted Jay, and the proof was in the results.

My father was also happy to play the link in the car shuffle game, driving us back and forth from wherever we had sailed to get us home for work, school, or doctor's appointments, or taking us to pick up our cars when they had been left at some remote location. He never complained, because he understood why we were doing it.

We received news that hit us like a ton of bricks: our six-year-old daughter Jennie was diagnosed with a severe case of lupus nephritis. In addition to all the other medical issues that come with the diagnosis, she could not get sunburned—ever. It was a matter of life and death. For a beach family it was a time of reckoning. What would we do? How would we cope as a family? Where could we move where there was no sun? How could she live an active life?

Unlikely as it seems, it turned out that the *Lotus* was our answer. Days spent on the *Lotus* weren't about sunning—they were about sailing.

Large sails meant lots of shady space on deck while little feet dangled over the sides. When there was no wind, the cabin below was perfect for reading, napping, and playing cards. We picked The Grand Hotel each spring because its massive oak trees covered every inch of the property with cool shade, their branches even sheltering parts of the pool and beach. We often visited nearby Pirate's Cove for the same reason, as oak trees shaded the swimming area there as well.

Closer to home we popped from one yacht club to another, sailed in the midday, and swam in the late afternoon when the sun was low on the horizon. The southerly sea breezes allowed us to fly down the waters just off the beach on a beam reach, the *Lotus's* preferred method of travel.

The northern Gulf Coast has some of the oldest yacht clubs in the United States, all scattered within a day's trip from Biloxi. Pass Christian claims to be older than the New York Yacht Club, which was established in 1844—this might not be technically true, but it's at least close. Biloxi was founded in 1849, Mobile in 1847, and the Southern Yacht Club in New Orleans was formed the same year as Biloxi.

It's not surprising that sailing took hold so long ago on the northern Gulf Coast, given the pleasant sea breezes that we have every afternoon in the late spring and summer. For centuries people from cities such as New Orleans and as far away as Chicago enjoyed the gentle winds that picked up offshore as the land masses heated up midday. Before the invention of air conditioning, wealthy people—and a few not so wealthy—built stately elevated homes with high ceilings, wide porches, and windows so tall that a person could walk through them. For good measure, builders added a long, wide hallway through the center of the house and called it a "dogtrot." This hallway along with transoms over doors and windows steered the southerly winds through all the rooms of the house.

Property owners at the time also added ornate pergolas in their front yards facing the beach to catch the breeze, often building them high up the base of a tree for the added shade. The height kept the landowners' delicate skin safe on those rare occasions that biting flies appeared, as the pests usually flew low to the ground. The pergolas were cleverly called "shoo-flies."

You don't hear about dogtrots and shoo-flies much anymore. They've been replaced by more boring terms—air conditioning and bug spray.

Chapter Three

*T*en years passed, and by the early nineties the boys were too tall to sleep on tiny bunks or the floor and Jennie wanted to bring friends on board. More importantly, I was tired of cleaning and sealing hot teak decks in a bikini on my two-week vacation. The *Lotus* had become our Velveteen Rabbit, and we nicknamed it the "Leaky Teaky" for good reason. It had melded our small family into a great sailing team, but they had outgrown the small boat and I had outgrown the tiny bikini. We had to have more space if we intended to keep the children sailing with us.

After a lot of waffling and a few goodbye tears, we sold the boat to a doctor who hired people to do the teak work for him. I never regretted our decision.

As Warren Buffet wisely said:

"Should you find yourself in a chronically leaking boat, energy devoted to changing vessels is likely to be more productive than energy devoted to patching leaks."

In an attempt to avoid all things teak, we moved up to a 32-foot Coronado with a center cockpit. It was a sturdy, safe boat, without much glamour, but with a lot of room below, and two heads. I don't even recall its name at this point, and only a few years later we happily sold it. I am pretty sure it was also happy to be rid of us. The separate staterooms for sleeping on opposite ends of the boat left way too much room for mischief and danger for the two boys and their sister, especially when the galley and food were on their end of the boat. Suddenly space was my enemy. The Coronado brings to mind another quote from Lin Pardey's book Bull Canyon, A Boat-Builder, a Writer, and Other Wildlife— "Thing about a boat is, you can always sell them if you don't like them. Can't sell children."

We kept the children.

Next came the 40-foot Irwin, *Encounter*, a sleeper of a boat. It took over my senses slowly with its perfect lay-out, easy maneuvering, and pretty looks. Different from the Cheoy Lee, which screams out its maker's name, this Ted Irwin-designed sailboat left people complimenting it and then asking, "what is it?"

While the *Lotus* loved a reach and could point, so did the faster Irwin, which made sailing to the barrier islands a lot easier.

I grew to love *Encounter* in the same way that older couples grow to love each other. There was nothing I would change, from the perfect galley to the friendly cockpit steps. It had no teak decks and little bright work to be varnished. Instead, it had lots of open deck space and a classy interior, with navy upholstery embroidered with bright gold stars. There was nothing the boat lacked for my purposes.

It fit me like a glove—cocktail parties after work on Fridays, summer sails that made me dream of never returning to port, and a sense of steadiness and predictability in the difficult years when our daughter was ill.

Like all our other boats the Irwin was docked at the Biloxi Small Craft Harbor, a location that enabled us to be sailing in a matter of minutes. It was only after a few years that we bought a small house on the river with a dock, and we permanently moved it to the safety of the Back Bay of Biloxi. We had two enormous pilings driven into the muddy bottom to secure the boat safely in the event of a hurricane.

The boys were growing into men by now, and in college Harrison started taking the Irwin on trips across the Gulf Coast with his friends and without us, often melding sailing and fishing into one adventure. His roommates had a large, framed picture of the *Encounter* prominently displayed on their living room wall. I slowly became more of a passenger, as the first mate roles were assumed by the young adults. The Irwin was still wonderful, just different. There were no more dockings for me, just relaxing. It was a great life—until it wasn't.

It wasn't a violent death, although Katrina tried its best. The Irwin simply floated over the top of its twenty-foot pilings and landed at the back door of a neighbor's home, ironically saving the home from the waves of the flood waters. I'd like to think it just pointed in that direction.

The insurance company insisted that *Encounter* would have to be dismembered and hauled away like some disloyal cartel member. The thing about a great boat, though, is that you can beat it up and turn it upside down, and it will still re-invent itself.

When I found out the insurance company sold our sailboat to someone else who repaired her, I was heartbroken. And I behaved like it. I searched on Google to find the new owner's name and then stalked him on road-trips to other harbors, secretly hoping that I would find both the boat and owner. I envisioned that he and the boat would look ragged out, sorry they had ever met. Eventually, I saw them in a New Orleans marina, albeit not together.

It wasn't at all what I had been guiltily wishing for. The Irwin looked great, hull gleaming just like the old days, and she seemed comfortable in her new slip and town. I was happy for her new life. However, when I stopped to talk to her, she pretended not to remember me. I knew then it was time to move on.

Candidly, I must admit that we had lost everything we owned in Katrina, and I was a tad bitter. I would have no more sailboats—and no more house either, or accompanying view of the water. We spent some nights evacuating in a condominium at Gulf Shores, and I refused to look out at the nearby waters that had betrayed me.

One day, a year after the hurricane and while Gulf cities were still wringing their hands over issuing building permits to reconstruct homes, I decided that we'd get a powerboat and live on it. The children were all grown or off at college. It was perfect timing. Maybe we'd buy an older classic Hatteras with lots of room—a fixer-upper that we could afford.

My immediate family said "sure, why not?" They all had enough worries of their own and weren't interested in listening to my whining. Only my younger brother, Doug, a yacht broker, tried to humor me by taking me to view boat after boat to find what I wanted.

That was until he saw that I was really going to buy one. He decided it was time to stop the madness.

He told me that he wouldn't participate in selling me the boat. Like a true best friend, he pointed out that my intended purchase was a rebound decision, not one based upon logic or even real love, one I was truly going to regret when I had to evacuate the large boat for a hurricane. Jay and I were not engine people or power boaters, and where were we going to keep it anyway?

Shoulders slumped and almost despondent, I walked away from the deal.

I was born in Biloxi, where my father was born and his father before him, and so on for well over a hundred years, despite the hurricanes that always seem destined for our front beach. Almost none of my ancestors left the counties where they were born—I'm not sure why. All I know is that I didn't leave either, even though for much of my life, I often dreamed of escaping.

It never happened. Like a summer storm, the desire to escape always managed to fade away whenever Jay and I sailed across the waters in front of our home in the late afternoon sun, nothing else around but gentle breezes, and silence—no phones, no Internet, no news – sometimes just a child's head in my lap as we lay under the shade of a sail. I had stayed and raised my family, built my career on the Gulf Coast, and invested my energies into one place.

A hurricane wouldn't make me leave.

We built a concrete house high on a bluff over the Tchoutacabouffa River after insurance paid what little it did. I didn't intend to lose two houses. Eventually my mood swings were mollified with various small powerboats. The small powerboats were fine, but we didn't even give them a name. They were only entertainment…not the civilized passion that sailing was for me. As the children began their independent lives, the boats became less entertainment and more yard ornaments.

I began to wonder what the rest of my life was destined to be. Work had been rewarding, especially as a school board attorney overseeing the construction of new schools in the city, and later, the construction of the Frank Gehry designed Ohr museum. But it was time for the stress and over-work to end. I needed a new chapter to begin.

Chapter Four

L ife takes crazy turns, and about the time that I was reconciled to a new normal, my husband Jay—the same man who saved me from a watery death in Key West, and probably many more times on other sailboats where I didn't know enough to be scared—that same man was offered a dream job with the U.S. State Department in Eastern Europe.

"Will you go?" he asked me.

I packed my bags.

It was the right time. The previous ten years had been intense, between mine and Jay's career, Jennie's health, the losses of my parents and brother, and the destruction of our every possession in Katrina. As much as I loved Biloxi, I needed some distance, some space in order to fully recover. As it was, everything at home still reminded me of what I had lost.

I realized that the seductive quiet islands off our shores were a jeweled chain with enough give to let me roam abroad, not a tether to keep me locked in place. They'd be there, along with my family, when I returned.

We lived in Romania and traveled all over the region, visiting Croatia, Hungary, Albania, Bosnia Herzegovina, Turkey, Montenegro, Greece, Serbia, Macedonia (now Northern Macedonia), Moldova, Ukraine, and everywhere in between. That meant, though, that for over two years our boating was on hold, unless you count taking a six-car ferry across the Danube. I could do nothing other than longingly watch yachting races on Sunday mornings on International CNBC, as the prospect of sailing was now just dinner conversation with new European friends in a different world.

The only thing that could have made it better was a boat.

One early spring day we were sipping a bold local red wine with friends at an outside café overlooking Bucharest's Lake Herastrau, watching the sunset, when the issue of "cash for clunkers" came up. (You might be wondering where this is heading, but bear with me.)

We had traded in our old gas-guzzling Jeep for a $2,500 credit before leaving the states. Ironically, we bought another, even older Jeep from an exiting diplomat in Romania and gave our gas tax money to that country instead.

In response to our "cash for clunkers" car story, our friends told us that the European Union, a bit late to develop a similar stimulus plan to revive its economy, was offering outrageous incentives to entice people to buy Beneteau sailboats, which are made in France. Undeniably, it was a program far more chic than our depressing-sounding "cash for clunkers." And the more that we sipped wine and the more we talked, the more it became clear that we needed to partake in this dignified method of boosting the French economy. It sounded like a simple enough plan—our EU friends would be the buyers and we would be partners. We would get it so cheaply it would be like robbery.

Beyond that we had no plans as to what we would do with the boat when it arrived. Unfortunately, you cannot sail a Beneteau on Lake Herastrau in Bucharest, Romania. It's a large lake, but shallow and only suited for Olympic rowers.

We left Europe after our tour with no Beneteau—it wasn't as easy as we thought to qualify for that gem of a program. I'm not even sure they had enough Beneteaus in the world for all the would-be owners, especially if lowly people like Jay and I were trying to get in the game. Instead, we went back stateside and back to reality: working, fishing, swimming, and experiencing a more laid-back life, in general. I occasionally worked part-time but spent most of my time nesting at home on the river.

The sense of space and time away had allowed us to remember all the reasons why we loved our home and were willing to stick with it, no matter the weather risks. The only thing missing at this point was boating: we still had no sailboat, and we weren't even looking for one.

It took a call from our friends in Romania the next year to jolt us back into the game.

"Forget buying a Beneteau," they said. They had chartered a 42 foot Lagoon catamaran in Croatia and asked us to join them for a week.

It took less than three seconds for us to say "yes," and our bags were packed the next day.

For the next three years we flew from Biloxi to Croatia every summer, sometimes twice, where we joined our Romanian friends for leisurely chartered sails around the Adriatic, hopping from island to island in the most civilized manner, with a captain and delicious Eastern European wines. We even sailed in the Adriatic Regatta, a decadent three-day race of Lagoons across the islands of Croatia, complete with seven-course meals and fully-stocked wine cabinet. It was the first time that Jay and I were able to observe very wealthy sailors from around the world. It was a huge undertaking for our hosts, something we couldn't have done without them.

During one of those Croatia trips our life changed direction once again. The friends called us a few months before we left, saying that in order to sail into Montenegro the charter boat needed two captains.

"Is Jay a captain?"

It was then that I had the great epiphany. I wanted Jay to retire, and he didn't want to leave his great career. He told me that he would only retire if he had something to do that challenged him. This, I decided, was it. I only needed to convince him to get his captain's license—and he had less than two months to do it.

Our son Patrick already had his captain's license and proceeded to run Jay through the process at full speed; medicals, drug tests, background tests, applications, and the hardest part, securing a spot in the last available captain's course. Three weeks later Jay was in a ten-day captain's course in Bayou LaBatre, Alabama, sleeping in a bunk with twenty other men, all in the tugboat industry, and wondering what in the world I had talked him into. Two weeks before we left for Croatia, Jay had his TWIC card, granting him access to ports around the world, and his captain's license.

Over the years Jay had logged the required hours needed to even be considered a captain—in his case it would be in the thousands. We sailed the Gulf Coast from one end to the other every year for forty years and logged many miles around the Adriatic. Jay grew up sailing on a Sunfish and sailed up the entire east coast on a trimaran after college. In addition to the Wednesday-night races and summer trips on the sailboats we owned, Jay raced on a Pearson with the Gulf Ocean Racing Circuit while I towed our children from city to city for the festivities. One cold year we flew to Nantucket where he raced with two others on the smallest boat in the famed Figawi race.

Another year we chartered an Erickson for three days with friends in San Diego and sailed in the Pacific, whales alongside. Then there were the trips in the Virgin Islands and Nova Scotia—and on it goes. Together we might not have sailed around the world in an epic trip, but we had logged tens of thousands of miles while juggling careers and family. To us this was a more epic story.

Even so, all our sailboat trips had one downside in common: they all had an end date. The end of the out-of-town seminar. The end of vacation. The end of our funds. I dreamed of the day when our lives wouldn't be controlled by end dates.

The new career I envisioned for Jay was the answer to those dreams. I hoped it would come in tandem with our latest sailboat purchase: the *Gypsy Lady*.

Chapter Five

We didn't name our Bermuda 40 MKIII Hinckley *Gypsy Lady*, but those who did, understood her well. One only needed to take the helm for a minute to know that she loved to run with the wind on a broad reach and flirt with the imaginations of seasoned sailors. She did it with me when I first saw her sitting forlorn in a slip on Mobile Bay, a bay she had not left in almost ten years. I could have sworn she saw me stop and look, my mouth open in wonder, and then she winked at me, begging for me to find her owner and make him an offer he couldn't resist. She was ready to be loosed from her muddy dock lines and mildewed fenders, and the sun showered her with potential.

I stood before her spellbound and called Jay.

"What do you think of her?" he asked from his government office at work, with its window view of the Gulf torturing him slowly each day that he sat confined in the twelve-by-twelve space that qualified as a premium office. I was standing on the docks of a neighboring yacht club filled with a hundred boats—from the sublime to the sinking—the still water reflecting the pilings and hulls in mirror images. It was a quiet morning, the sun on my face and fresh air in my lungs.

I stood on the sailboat's finger piers, judged her length, marveled at her sea-kindly lines and wide-open decks, and peeked inside the windows at the mahogany walls and sturdy, curving craftsmanship inside. But it was the small, almost sexy stern, sitting high up above the water line, that caused me to lose control of my senses like some aphrodisiac. I sent pictures to Jay. I might have fallen in love with another woman, but I knew that we had to have the *Gypsy Lady*.

Elvis Presley's words of warning— "only fools rush in and fall in love"—went unheeded. There was only one person to convince that I was right, and he was in the mood to dream, not work. A few minutes later I called Jay and relayed the information that I had found; she was for sale. This wasn't a surprise, because as most boaters know, all boats are for sale at the right price. That "right price" was a stretch for us—the most we had ever spent on any one thing besides a house—but good timing and overwhelming desire made it possible.

Our purchase is really the story of the second owner, however, not the first. And the story of her first owners should be told now, not later.

I know the names of the original owners in 1980, their perfect penmanship, their dreams of places like Antigua, Nova Scotia, and Bermuda, and their meticulous record-keeping in detailed blue binders that were passed down to us. What I may never know is what made them un-love her. How did *Gypsy Lady* betray them, I wonder—because that's the only thing it could be—such that they put her up on a shameful wooden platform in a commercial boatyard for ten years and never sailed on her again?

They were a young couple in 1980, with enough money to special order the premier sailing boat in the U.S., specially made from the yard, including extravagant extras such as banquette seating, Chelsea clock, and barograph made in Paris. The four-hour chime clock for watches and continuous marking barograph still works, and the device's extra lead and graph paper still fill the chart table as if frozen in time. In fact, *Gypsy Lady* is as intact today as she was when commissioned, hull number 174, one of a few dozen sloops of her kind built at the Hinckley Shipyard in Southwest Harbor, Maine. Not only did the first owners know how to name a boat, but they also knew how to buy the best.

It also struck me as something wonderful that the wife was an integral part of the purchase, with copies of technical letters to and from the factory in her hand. I especially appreciated the dignity with which the factory responded. The Hinckley staff understood that sailing is genderless, and women do it as well as men—agility and brains are needed, not brawn. Winch handles and a windlass are great equalizers.

Over the years the two previous owners made repairs so subtle that they were almost invisible, and they never considered removing the original wood walls in the head due to over-used showers, installing granite countertops (and really, who would do that?), or worse, drilling invasive holes for electronics long past their prime. *Gypsy Lady* didn't even have a paper towel holder.

Maybe the years of storage restrained the *Gypsy Lady*'s desires, but its owners kept her alive, bones in perfect shape. Much like someone who wears sunscreen every day, she avoided the pitfalls of over-use.

The second owner we know. He loved the *Gypsy Lady* as if it were a part of him. He knew the boat from bow to stern, and I imagine that he whispered to her of the places they might one day go, but the *Gypsy Lady* is very complicated and demanding—and sometimes that becomes too much. They never took the trip. When we came around it was time to give her up to new lovers.

I doubt that's why the first owners sold her. It had to be either a harrowing experience or hurricane, or both. Maybe it was the spouse who refused to leave the boat in a storm. The boat is so tender—with its curved belly, it heaves toward the sea before reaching equilibrium, or frantically races ahead of the building waves to search for safety. Maybe it was seeing a hurricane destroy the docks so lovingly built to protect *Gypsy Lady*, perfectly constructed corsets that within seconds disintegrated into nothing. Or maybe it was none of the above—just a new love for them. One not so risky, so exhilarating, or so needy.

Given the frequency and timing of hurricanes I guess it was some combination of "all of the above." And whatever it was, we were clearly its beneficiaries.

As beautiful as *Gypsy Lady* was with all her minor time-inflicted imperfections, shortly after our purchase we quickly discovered that her lack of air conditioning was the one thing that absolutely had to be remedied. Mid-day summer sun in a slip was intolerable.

That installation meant hauling the boat out for a thru-hull fitting, which as all boaters know, meant that once on the yard "we might as well…" keep going, until every tiny screw was replaced, and every inch painted or varnished. Soon enough, the *Gypsy Lady* looked as if she were just christened.

During the boatyard work we made a firm decision that we would continue with the previous owners' plans, making no changes from the boat's original commissioning. No paper towel holders or TVs on the walls, no color change, and the retro cassette/radio player still remains, singing its tunes.

While the workers focused on the outside, I emptied the storage areas and enjoyed logging in everything that the previous owners had left (which was a replacement for nearly every filter, belt, shackle, or other part we might need). Then I restocked it all. I have always been the one asked to find a tool, screw, or bolt in a matter of seconds, so I stored everything where it made sense to me. It was so effective that Jay named it the "two-second plan", as I could find anything within two seconds.

I don't want to give the impression that just because Jay was elevated to captain, that I was demoted to the role of his first mate. I just happened to be more organized. It's a common assumption that wives are either hood ornaments or deck hands—an idea promoted even during our only joint sailing class—but as I told friends, "Jay may be the captain, but I am the owner." I'd take the helm whenever I wanted it.

By the end of 2019 the boat was like new. *Gypsy Lady* was back on the water and charters were beginning to fill the calendar. Then the calendar flipped to 2020 and COVID happened; and happened, and happened.

I had rarely been on *Gypsy Lady* before for any purpose other than the restoration. When she became sidelined, it was easy to become disengaged from her as she sat idle in the slip. I began to resent the fact that I had never once spent the night on her away from the dock. Because of COVID I couldn't go to the national parks on the barrier islands.

For all of 2020, the *Gypsy Lady* sat in her boat slip confined to a rectangular void of still, dark water delineated only by four pilings, tethered to each like a corralled racehorse, pulling and groaning against her captivity each time the wind picked up. And pick up the wind did, but when it really blew, she would suffer more humiliation, forced to motor inland, sails constrained, searching for safety from one hurricane hole to another to avoid the five major storms that visited the Gulf of Mexico that year.

I began to wonder if I was getting too old and we had bought her too late. After all, it was a big boat for the two of us. The boys had been with us on most trips on our last boats, but now they were married with lives of their own. Everything about the Lady was complicated and, to me, counter intuitive.

Why, for example, would they put the most important parts of the engine, which sometimes need two people to access for maintenance, in the most difficult place? Not just one time, but seemingly every time? And why was the galley designed for someone six feet tall? It was always a tad too high for me to see out of a window or too deep a locker for me to reach into. In fact, both the refrigerator and the cabinet behind it were large enough to carry a dead body. In the beginning I was reluctant to put my hand all the way inside the food cabinet for fear that an animal could be lurking below in the dark.

It began to irritate me. So what if Rockefeller and the owner of Conde Naste had Hinckleys too? How tall were they anyway?

As 2020 droned on, I tried to forget the trips to Europe, the parties, and the Mardi Gras parades that we had to cancel, and I tried hard to be a good sport. Holidays came and went, and we stayed inside, mostly just the two of us huddled in front of the television, Jay no longer working and undoubtedly wishing that he was.

But not everyone stayed home like good troopers—including two of our friends who went to a large family Christmas party in Atlanta. (Yes, they all got COVID.) We offered them our house in which they could isolate and get well, and decided that for those few days we would stay on the boat in the harbor. It would be cozy, perhaps even romantic. News got out quickly about our gratuitous plan. Rumors grew on some variation that "Jay and Patti are taking off for a long sailboat trip somewhere exotic." Forget romance—we were headed for a great adventure.

Really? In January with north winds and freezing temperatures and only a day or two of planning?

Immediately, bored friends and family were practically throwing us bon voyage parties when we only planned to hang out close to home, preferably in a slip with electricity and Internet. It was as if they were yelling "jump, jump" while we were up on the high dive, goading us to go in head-first or be deemed cowards. I dearly love these people, but I know they wouldn't leave their king-size beds and down comforters in January. Even worse, they'd be the first to say we should have known better when we came home with frostbite.

Chapter Six

*T*he problem was that on January 3rd the wind direction was too good, the skies too clear, and the waters too perfect to avoid leaving town, if not for a week, then perhaps a few days. Spontaneous sailing decisions weren't unusual for us, but until that day COVID had stymied us. But, really, what better way to be isolated from others who were ill than being out at sea?

We cooked a couple of meals and did minimal provisioning, and then packed a bit of warm clothing, telling ourselves not to over-pack—it never stays cold for long. Our plan was to drop anchor at a nearby island one night and then wander around for a few days, seeking shelter in existing marinas when we could.

At the last minute on the way to the harbor I thought about the light-weight fleece blankets on board and suggested that we pick up some sleeping bags for those nights we slept at anchor without any heat.

"For 50-degree weather or 30?" I asked Jay as we looked at all the options in the local outfitter store. It didn't feel that cold outside. The 30-degree sleeping bag cost more, and how often does it go below 40 at night on the Gulf Coast?

"Let's go with 30," he said. "Probably not necessary, but it isn't that much more."

I nodded in agreement, like I had spent many days contemplating this decision.

"30 it is."

Do I need to tell anyone what a great decision that was?

It does, in fact, freeze on the Gulf Coast. It did just that for the first two weeks of our trip, even icing the decks some mornings. Freezing temperatures on the water with a north wind feel ten times colder than on land, and most boats are not insulated. Days like these can chill you to the bone, making you feel like a reality-TV star hunkered down in a sleeping bag in a log cabin in the Arctic Circle, shivering with a flashlight in hand and recording just how miserable you are…but still trying to convince everyone else that it's a wonderful life.

We ultimately resorted to using the inverter for heat, but by the time that happened we as were as cold-hardy as Grizzly Adams, and I had become adept at cooking a hot meal at breakfast and dinner to warm the cabin.

I've mentioned that 2020 was a year of hurricanes, but I have so far omitted the havoc that they wreaked on the northern Gulf Coast as a whole. Each little port town suffered similar fates, with marinas and docks destroyed, homes and businesses with walls and roofs ripped off, and water intrusion everywhere. Add COVID to the mix and it was a sad situation.

The storms and their damage combined to make one continuous disaster site across the coast in four states, but before taking this trip we only knew our own misfortunes. Residents of one city are unable to concentrate on the troubles a different storm might have wrought in another coastal town when they have their own peculiar issues to manage. The enormity of what we didn't know would not sink in until much later.

That lack of knowledge reminded me of an expensive sailing class I took to get some certificate that I later realized was meaningless. The entire class was spent on those things that I had already learned from sailing for thirty-plus years, so I spent most of the two days observing the other four classmates on the 20-foot Catalina proclaim their vast wealth of knowledge gleaned from bloggers on the Internet. None of the four men had ever sailed in Gulf waters, but fully intended to sail the world the next year—in their own boats that they did not yet own.

In fact, they were so full of confidence that they were compelled to explain everything to me even though they never managed to master the art of tying a dock line to a cleat. They mistook my late-afternoon quiet for a lack of knowledge. The truth was that after endless "man overboard" drills to retrieve a floating orange life vest in record heat on a windless bay, all I could think about was a cold drink on shore.

Jay knew that the instructor was wasting his time on the lesson. He loved to tell the story that despite the many successful "man overboard" drills we had practiced on our 27-foot Cheoy Lee, the only time one of our children did fall overboard, I jumped in immediately afterwards. Suddenly, Jay had only small children on the boat and was tasked with plucking two people out of the gulf, not one.

He claims that no amount of training is sufficient to overcome maternal or familial instinct, and offers my story as anecdotal proof in support of the military's practice of forbidding brothers from serving in the same unit. In war, survival often depends upon an automatic training response, but family loyalties could undermine the desired outcome.

"It doesn't matter that she was fully dressed; she jumped in right behind the child who fell overboard," he'd say, shaking his head.

I hadn't changed over time. Each time the instructor referred to the life vest as a baby, I'd cock my head and look at him as if he were insane. There's no way I'd overcome my maternal instinct to save my child.

The four men didn't know each other before the class but were connected by their devotion to the current boating trend of "quit your job and go sailing around the world." The fact that their wives weren't in the class with them told me a lot about the probability of that occurring, but I'm sure they missed those signs.

Listening to them pontificate for hours about what it was going to be like on their world voyage was often entertaining. It was impossible to give them any input that might dent their enthusiasm, especially when bloggers made it seem so easy and the sailing school was pitching pricey upgraded sailing packages for people just like them.

At the end of the day, their youthful confidence won me over and we hugged good-bye. I genuinely wished them well on their grand trips; I had a feeling they would need it.

I only point out this story because there was one golden rule that the instructor constantly repeated that applies to all new sailors—the rule that I knew the future world-trippers didn't yet fully appreciate and wouldn't for years: Local knowledge trumps everything. It doesn't matter what the chart says if last week the sands shifted, markers changed, the bridge is locked in place due to mechanical problems, or the fuel docks in the next port are closed for leaks.

To receive the most current information you should talk to a real person—someone with that all-too-often indefinable quality of experience. The best source is the boat that's just passed through the area you are about to enter, especially on the Intracoastal Waterway. But, as I would learn later, this too can fail you.

It was usually my job to wave at a passing boater, compliment their boat, and then, if they engaged in conversation, to ask if the bridge up ahead was stuck again and see if they offer any unsolicited advice about the way forward. Was there anything else we should know before pushing ahead? Were markers missing? All the cool electronics and the fastest Internet in the world can't put your boat back together again when you suddenly hit a sunken craft before it has been properly marked.

Especially after a hurricane, local knowledge is critical.

We spent the first night of our COVID venture in our local stomping grounds. We anchored at Petit Bois Island, one of four pristine islands off Mississippi owned by Jay and I. Well, maybe we didn't exactly own them— they were officially managed by the National Park Service as part of the Gulf Islands National Seashore, but there is so much open space you can always find a spot to be alone.

There we enjoyed the first night of what would be weeks of showy sunsets, bursting across the horizon in the short days after the winter solstice. The white sandy beaches on the island's north shore surround a pretty cove that provides a great anchorage safe from the Intracoastal traffic as well as protection from the wind on the island's lee side.

We reluctantly left Petit Bois early in the morning, at the first glimmer of light, knowing that we would have to use every minute of daylight in that short day to cross Mobile Bay.

We planned to stop the second night in another perfect anchorage, Ingram Bayou, Alabama, on the Intracoastal Waterway east of Mobile. It was a great plan, but the day sailing across the Mobile Bay was cold and long, and by dark we were tired. Although we had a nice beam reach with a northerly wind, the current was against us, making the trip much slower than we wanted, especially on a day short on sunlight.

The only ship we had encountered in the two days since we left Biloxi was a confusing mirage—an other-worldly wooden ship headed toward us, its edges blurred by a light surrounding fog. Ultimately, it turned out to be the Pinta headed to its next tourist stop (without Columbus). I was greatly relieved to see that it was only a replica of the famous boat emerging in the fog, and not actually a ghost ship—although it was a sign of things to come. Why else would Columbus be in Mobile Bay during the time of COVID?

Our solitude continued for the first two days and then for most of the next four weeks—we never crossed the path of another sailor when we were in the open Gulf. We saw two freighters but no barges, as they generally moved at night. Patrick, our son, insisted that once there were two other sailboats in our vicinity according to the AIS tracking system, but we never saw any evidence that they existed in anything other than cyberspace.

Sometimes we were so alone that I began to wonder if the world had ended and we didn't know it. If we wanted space away from people, we had found it. The spotty cell phone coverage didn't help.

That is why it was so shocking when we entered the Intracoastal Waterway in Alabama. Late on a Sunday afternoon it was anything but quiet, swarming with boats full of cold, happy families bundled up in blankets. Suddenly staying alone in Ingram Bayou at anchor lost its appeal, and we found ourselves caught in the honey-sweet fly trap known as Lulu's.

The incredibly convenient and enticing Lulu's Restaurant in Alabama is a guilty pleasure for those trying to avoid unhealthy food. Lulu herself is best known as Jimmy Buffet's sister, and her restaurant is known for its cheeseburgers and fun music—a sprawling entertainment center for families arriving in cars or boats. Her marina is convenient and perfect for transients.

We told ourselves that we wouldn't stop there for showers or food. In fact, we wouldn't eat out at all due to COVID, as no one had vaccines yet at this point and we weren't going to risk anything. No, we were there for a more noble purpose; the stop would enable us to pick up some transmission fluid from a nearby marine store before pushing further east.

But Lulu's had more than just the perfect location to snare unsuspecting boaters like us; it doubled down on its charms by sending out Jimmy Buffet music and the aroma of fried food wafting over our bow. We caved too easily. In less than an hour after securing the boat, we found ourselves taking criminally-long hot showers to remove the lingering chill in our bones and succumbing to juicy hamburgers with a signature cocktail while sitting at a patio table (far away from other customers at least). We gazed in contentment at the Intracoastal Waterway, which was lit up in a spectrum of yellows and oranges from the sunset, as the band played on.

After we paid the check, we reluctantly agreed that as enjoyable as the dinner and our slip had been, we didn't want to get too comfortable. Spending the rest of our lives at Lulu's wasn't a great life plan.

Shrugging off the prior night's caloric intake, we left at daybreak toward Pensacola, my mother's family home and the site of all my childhood family vacations. It was important that we find a safe and secure slip and do it quickly, as NOAA predicted approaching severe weather with expected winds over 30 knots. The temperature would continue to hover just about freezing at night and in the fifties in the afternoon, but most days would be sunny at least, making it feel slightly warmer.

Both Jay and I read the brutally honest weather reports together and talked about the options. In the end we agreed that we needed to find shelter and needed it quickly.

Chapter Seven

$\mathcal{A}$ s we had done many times over the years, Jay and I meandered through islands and slits of land with sandy beaches made brilliant white in the afternoon sun, rounded the Naval Air Station in the Pensacola Bay, and turned our craft into the welcoming arms and contours of Bayou Chicot.

Pensacola Yacht Club sits proudly at the bayou's entrance, a constant symbol of historic beauty and resilience: white wood walls, expansive verandas, blue awnings, and a huge pool, looking much like it has for over a hundred years. It was already well on the way to total recovery after Hurricane Sally, but its transient slips were only for "lay-up," which meant that our boat would have little protection in the wind direction that was about to make an appearance.

Docking with bad wind direction can be a chore, but Jay and I have a well-rehearsed plan. In a city or private dock Jay uses the wind and a little bit of the engine to help maneuver *Gypsy Lady* to where she will ultimately dock. Then, as soon as a piling or cleat is reachable, I wrap the cleat with a line or, if necessary, I simply hug the piling closest to the boat's center to keep it in place until the boat's engine and forward movement stop. Once the boat is safely in the slip, we both take opposite dock lines, adjust the line lengths, and then cleat them off, both of us knowing by habit the way to secure her. We're fast, but still, it takes a bit of effort.

Entering the yacht club marina, we reduced speed to enter a slip. A few members ambled out of the clubhouse to see the newest entry, cocktails in hand. I only needed to throw them a line and they did the rest.

We stayed one night, but in that short time we made fast friends with the owner of the Hatteras across the boat launch from us, who crazily knew many of the same people we did at home. He had tested positive for COVID and was isolating on his yacht. The distance across a boat launch between us made it ideal for social distancing—complete with evening cocktails—and we hated to leave, but we knew it was time to retreat further into the bayou.

The wind was picking up from the southeast, the worst direction considering where our boat was moored, so we left the good conversation and comforts of the yacht club. Without a line attached to a piling or other protection on the windward side, the boat's hull on the opposite side would be crushed up against the pier.

The weather was also forecasted to be cold for the foreseeable future. The northern Gulf Coast from Louisiana to Tallahassee has a temperate climate in the winter, which normally equates to a few days near freezing followed by a few days when you use air conditioning, rotating like this until Lent. January 2021 was proving to be the exception, with the normal lows, but not the welcomed highs. It was important to me that we be in the bayou and avoid the added sting of the direct wind.

We had always assumed that Bayou Chicot was the best hurricane hole on the coast, and if we had a million or two, we would buy a house and dock for our boat. My cousin Tommy has lived our dream for forty years in a small, cool bungalow high up a hill overlooking the bayou. When we called to let him know that we were in Pensacola, he reminded us that his dock and boat had been destroyed during the hurricane, but thankfully his house was intact. That news meant we'd have to find somewhere else to dock. He tried to convey the level of damage in the rest of the bayou from Hurricane Sally, but it's hard to understand the extent of each hurricane's destruction until you see it for yourself.

The slow lonely crawl of our sailboat that gray morning into the bayou was ominous. We were quieted by scenes of boats scattered about like discarded toys, some stranded high on land and others sunk in marshy shallows. Docks looked like piles of loose toothpicks interspersed with white lines and broken power cords. The winter low tide and flapping torn sails made boats lying on their sides in the mud look like bombed-out warships, abandoned and left for dead on the cold, dark day. The hurricane had been almost four months earlier.

Boats in Bayou Chicot weren't alone in their demise. The beautiful new downtown harbor in the city center of Pensacola suffered worse: it was totally gone. Boats that did not evacuate simply tore the piers away or landed on other boats in a tangle of lines that doomed them and the docks to a collective destruction.

Getting a transient slip for more than a night was difficult, no matter who you knew. When we finally were able to secure a slip for two nights at the Pensacola Shipyard, our view included million-dollar boats that were forlornly sitting on "the hard," uneasily squeezed between stands, with their enormous gashes, broken masts, and big insurance company stickers signifying a total loss.

It was humbling. *Gypsy Lady* had suffered damage in Zeta, but it was cosmetic and not so vicious. How quickly had I forgotten the power of the weather gone bad and our own losses in Katrina?

One of the few other boats lucky enough to be repairable and to have a functioning slip with power was a 52-foot Island Packet owned by excellent local sailors David and Mary. In less than three days we bonded as fellow sailors usually do, especially when twice we were the beneficiaries of their stellar cooking. It is only natural that, as sailors so often do over several bottles of fine wine, it didn't take long to plan a trip to the Bahamas together.

Why go home to Biloxi? Keep sailing, we thought to ourselves.

That's what our family and friends had implied from the start. So far *Gypsy Lady* had exhibited no desire to head home in shame, and Jay and I found we were getting the best sleep of our lives, rocking like babies in the cozy berths. Why not keep on?

It was a loose plan, like the planned Beneteau purchase, and basically went like this: we'd meet up with Mary and David later in the winter in south Florida to take the crossing to the Bahamas. If they could do it, so could we.

We didn't simply laze away while the wind howled around us at the edge of the shipyard, however. Outside of his real work, our youngest child Patrick served as a 24 /7 free tele-boat mechanic for us, and we took the three-day opportunity to overnight a new water pump for our not-so-new Westerbeke engine. We had reported to him some unusual sounds that we were hearing and he felt it was a necessary item to be handled before we continued our journey. Early Tuesday morning he guided Jay through its installation via iPhone. In a matter of minutes it was time to leave the slip, which as we were repeatedly told by the marina office, we had over-stayed. We were off to Destin, a little over forty years since our Key West trip.

Destin Harbor, from its '70s identity as a small fishing cove to a now-famous summer playground, seems to have a makeover every ten years or so. The fragile and narrow slip of land between the Gulf and bays is so valuable that nowadays even a hugely popular restaurant can wake up to find itself being bulldozed to the ground for a newer, glitzier, and perhaps ten times taller building, one so high it looms above the harbor: growth fueled not by need, but by greed, some real estate developer's lust for fresh money.

Those changes do not bode well for many sailors crossing the northern Gulf Coast. The bridges to the calmer and expansive waters of the Choctahatchee Bay are too low and do not swing wide or lift open. Even in Jay's and my small town, far less prosperous than Destin and Fort Walton, ample safe harbor waters are accessible for large sailboats. No matter how small the body of water or bridge, there is a kind bridge tender at some time of the day or week when needed in foul weather.

Why northwestern Florida politicians decided it would be a good idea to save money by constructing bridges of 50 feet in height rather than the standard 65 feet for marine traffic—thus dooming cruising sailors to the open Gulf in bad weather—is beyond my understanding. The incredibly busy Destin harbor basin is often a large sailboat's only option.

Transient slips in the harbor are rare, especially in a winter low tide, as the docks and piers with deep water are full of rental boats, jet skis, charter boats, kayaks, and any other floatable thing you can think to rent. Piers, fuel docks, and private marinas with hundreds of charter boats encroach so far into the remaining water that it feels like the walls of a pool closing in, forcing the boaters to move through the middle in tight little circles around each other. Even in the dead of winter, when tourists and fishermen are warm at home, hearty sailors have little room in which to safely drop anchor in the coveted deep waters of the inlet.

We dreaded Destin from past experiences like this, but found that in COVID January it was a pleasant surprise.

We arrived just at dusk, thrilled to see new jetties and a well-dredged channel with almost no traffic. If Destin was hit by the effects of any hurricane, it didn't show. The *Gypsy Lady* gently dropped anchor alongside three other sailboats which, we later learned, were caravanning together somewhere south. I'm not sure they were going anywhere soon, however, as they were all waiting for boat parts and, according to them, the boats had been there so long that they were already knowledgeable about the local lunch menus and on friendly terms with the post office employees.

Young and gregarious, the sailor on the nearby 30-foot Tartan motored his dinghy alongside us and kindly offered to take us ashore if we wanted provisions or to wander the docks. Despite my vow to eat on-board due to COVID, I almost relented until he pointed out that his dinghy leaked and held water in the bottom. We'd eat on board. I was a savvy provisioner after all my years of sailing. The day before we left for Florida I had made and frozen a white wine turkey tetrazzini casserole, as well as a large pot of chili, and bought eggs, cheese, bread, cereal, milk, and other food we could pull together in meals without stress. The boat was already stocked with condiments and spices. I knew we weren't going to starve or freeze to death at night.

The temperature outside was about forty degrees when our yachting neighbor waved a cheery good-bye and apologized in advance for his loud generator. I replied that it was no problem and, as I did, was momentarily startled by the fact that I hadn't really missed or even thought about our lack of a generator until that moment.

The *Gypsy Lady* is forty feet long but only about twelve feet across, the width similar to most fishing boats of the same length. The galley is to port, on the immediate left of the three steps which lead from the companionway to the salon. It has all the necessities of a nice kitchen in a fraction of the space. The galley also contains the best single item on *Gypsy Lady*—the gimbled stove, which stays level no matter how much the boat heels. Not only does it keep the contents on the stove or in the oven from spilling, it has the added bonus of heating the entire salon at night when the dinners are cooking and again in the morning when the coffee is brewing.

If the oven didn't warm us, using the engine would, or else the sun streaming through the windows during the day would do the trick. The whole interior, walls and storage, closets and drawers, is constructed like a fine piece of furniture with rounded edges, all brightened by the sky-blue upholstery on the endless seating options. It screams come lounge in me! —in a civilized manner, of course.

The dining, game-playing, writing, painting, and all-around fun area is an adjustable table that can serve a five-course dinner for up to eight people. It's surrounded on three sides by U-shaped banquette seating that was special ordered by the original owner, situated at the widest part of the beam of the boat. On the starboard side opposite it there are two full berths, one perfectly tucked up under the decks above and the other situated for seating at the dining table or pulled out to create a large berth. The dining table can be lowered to form another double bed as well.

Further towards the bow is a full head, hanging lockers, many drawers, and a privacy door which leads to the v-berth that sleeps two people comfortably.

It was a perfect lay-out for us on this trip, just wide enough to be roomy, but narrow enough to hold me upright when the water was rough, especially given all the convenient handholds.

Best of all, it was flexible. I like to say that two couples cruising or eight men racing can sleep comfortably on her.

Chapter Eight

S o far, there was nothing about the cozy evenings we spent on the trip that we didn't both enjoy; a glass of wine, cheese and cracker appetizers, a hot meal, reading, long talks about family, the day, and the people we met. It was so easy to take our time talking when there were no distractions.

At some point while in Pensacola, Jay and I fell into the habit of taking turns reading out loud chapters from a lengthy book, Hemingway's Boat: Everything He Loved in Life and Lost, 1934-1961, by Paul Hendrickson. The book, given to us by our friend Ronnie for the trip, is a fascinating look into Hemingway's life, but on that long cold evening in Destin, when dinner was over and we had talked ourselves out, something prompted Jay to suggest that we write our own longest sentence about the Destin Pass in order to rival Hemingway's 424-word sentence about the Gulf Stream. It's not like we didn't have a lot of time to do it, and the inspiration was right outside our window.

Jay lay back on the banquette seat that surrounded the table, hands behind his head and legs stretched out, to think about his masterpiece, and soon began to dictate his sentence to me. I sat across from him on a berth with a writing pad, pen in hand, like a secretary from the '50s.

It didn't take long for both of us to realize that our sentence was total nonsense, but he kept on and on and I suddenly found that I couldn't stop laughing. I had forgotten how painful uncontrolled laughing can be, and at that moment I recalled that you can die from laughter—and I told Jay that. I had married him because he made me laugh, and there I was on a sailboat, with a serious chance that I would be the only sailor to ever die from that little-known affliction. He had to stop writing. It was headed nowhere good.

Jay sat upright, sighed, and agreed. He abandoned his Hemingway writing career just for me.

At daylight the next morning we pulled anchor and fueled up along with the charter fishing boats. It was hard not to think about the fact that Destin Harbor was now too expensive and its beaches too exclusive for many people. Everything had changed since the '70s. Young boaters couldn't survive without generators, and older boaters seldom took out their boats apart from a few weeks in summer when everyone else also went out at once, milling around and anchoring in the confined waters.

Not us, though—we were ready to tackle sailing in the open Gulf further eastward.

Light north winds and abundant sunshine turned the sail from Destin to Panama City into a sight-seeing excursion of seashore parks, miles of long thin islands, and an endless series of expensive beach towns. With calm seas, a midday sun, and gentle beam reach, it was perfect timing to pull out the binoculars and observe the onshore scenery. We cruised by the beaches under the power of the jib, so close that we could easily watch the people and their pets in the rare times that they appeared. Homes were mostly vacant.

I found that even without a chart I could distinguish the planned communities from the other small beach towns that have organically grown over the past century. Newer and quite high-end, the former incorporated architectural elements based on Mediterranean villas, Carolina cottages, eclectic island beach chic, and other trendy aesthetics. They may look different from the roadway, but from our view they were all the same, matching each other in their coordinated soft color palettes, varying only slightly in square footage and height from one to the next, and never unnecessarily drawing attention to any single home.

Older and less accessible towns were a mixture of new mansions interspersed between dated one-story beach homes stubbornly retaining their original condition, along with other large, rambling homes that had grown like the limbs of an old oak tree, heavy odd additions here and there as the families living within them expanded.

The best towns had examples of new development mixed in with old and true north Florida construction methods: traditional weathered boards and batten homes with expansive screen porches, or smaller homes with painted concrete block walls and jalousie windows for summer breezes. They ranged from the glitzy to those in some stage of disrepair, and came in every color imaginable, but the homes always had verandas that didn't stop at any corner but rather lovingly encased the occupants on all sides.

I imagine that soon these homes will disappear too as the original owners pass away, the land becomes too valuable, and the heirs sell. Then no beach land will be left unturned by the bulldozers of developers vying for the money of the summer visitors from up north who want a home that looks like it's from anywhere else but the Panhandle.

I had lots of time to ponder who owned the exclusive homes in all these towns, and if anyone in them was watching our lone sailboat cross the horizon past their windows. Did they wish they were on *Gypsy Lady* under sail, quietly heading east, or wonder who we were and what exotic place we might go, or were they happy in their warm slippers and cozy chair with coffee in hand, gazing at the white sailboat on the blue-green Gulf as if they would look at a painting on their wall? Or did they not consider us at all, as if we were nothing but a random cloud passing by? I imagined it was the latter.

There was one lone runner on the beach who I knew observed us. I could tell it from the sideways glances and turn of his head in our direction, even from afar, as his long, even strides made dark shadows on the white sand. Then something clicked, as if he and *Gypsy Lady* were kindred souls, and he challenged her for a race with a slight nod of his head, his eyes boring into my binoculars. I immediately noticed an uptick in his speed: man against the boat, legs and lungs against sail and wind. In the beginning the race was even, but eventually the wind began to gust in our favor. I could almost hear the runner panting as he would look sideways at us and run even faster until for a moment, we were neck and neck. But the *Gypsy Lady* was not in it for the short haul. He was, however, eventually stopping and bending over, hands on his knees and catching his breath as he watched us pull away toward our next port.

I almost wished that he had won.

The transition from gentle cruising to entering unfamiliar ports can be jarring, but it wasn't when we entered Panama City. The deep and wide channel with large markers didn't compete with the flood of city lights. If anything, in January it was deceptively empty, almost as if we were entering an uninhabited city.

We intended to anchor in St. Andrews Bay, as the city marina was destroyed, but beyond that I was totally perplexed; the bay appeared on the guides as a not-too-big blob of water surrounded by Shell Island and the St. Andrews Park, and too close to the city to feel remote. But at that point there were no other options. It would have to do.

How wrong could I be? Not only was it a perfectly beautiful, safe, and deep anchorage, it was large enough to hold a fleet of aircraft carriers. It would have helped to have one other boat somewhere in the bay just to help force a decision as to where to drop anchor. Instead, we wandered around for what seemed like an hour in circles, like a dog seeking the optimum time to drop down, ultimately choosing the spot with the best sunset view and wind direction. We told ourselves that next time, when it was warmer, we would drop anchor closer to the beach.

The downtown city lights were so far away that I wasn't sure there was a city at all. The light glow from towering condos at Panama City Beach was even further away, dulled by distance or masked by tree lines from the park, making me wonder if they were suddenly vacant. The lack of ambient light was disorienting because I knew Panama City existed. I had been there. Where had it gone?

We were totally alone in a spectacular bay with a moonless, starry sky and endless dark horizons, a glass of red wine and a hot meal. Where but on the Gulf Coast could you anchor so close to land and yet feel such a remoteness and absolute quiet? And then wake up the next morning to find yourself once again in the middle of a blue bay, surrounded by pristine white sand dunes, cloudless skies, and no one else?

Jay and I had been alone for much of 2020 because of COVID, taking walks and picking blackberries, but after we made twenty bottles of fruit wine and completed a dozen puzzles, we ran out of fun things to do. Sailing alone under the circumstances was a totally new experience: challenging, but rejuvenating. We were able to laugh at our earlier sailing experiences, laugh over words in Scrabble, and make ridiculous bets playing poker. We planned for the future and appreciated our past. It was a time for dreaming and we soaked it in, as we knew that it would, sooner or later, end. What more could we wish for?

Possibly one might wish for warmer days. It was another freezing morning with ice on the decks when we left the channel and went east toward Apalachicola, and by that point I was tired of being a good sport about our lack of warm clothes. I probably was never a good sport about it, but I did the best I could layering thin pants over tights and covering my feet with multiple pairs of thin socks inside my warmest shoes: topsiders. Socks served as gloves and were not exactly good for warmth or sailing. I made a goal right then—I intended to go shopping in Apalachicola for Arctic clothes, the sooner the better. No stopping along the way.

Chapter Nine

*T*here were two options to get from Panama City to Apalachicola, and both required that we continued to sail at least half-way on the "outside" in the open Gulf, which meant there would be no protected harbor in the event of bad weather or mechanical issues.

Option One was to go the entire trip outside and Option Two was to go outside for the first half, then take the five-mile cut that opened along the coastline roughly half the distance to Apalachicola. The cut was just west of Port St. Joe, whose lone city harbor had been annihilated in Hurricane Sally. The quaint city's broad empty basin was only inhabited by winter's white pelicans along with a smattering of gray. I used the word "annihilated" because at this point I have run out of descriptions for what looks like the results of a bombing raid.

The cut wasn't only more protected, but a far shorter distance than running outside the entire way, and the short days made time of the essence. Only an America's Cup boat would have chosen Option One on that windy day. I feel sure that if they did, they would find the thirty-knot gusts from the north quite invigorating.

We left at daybreak to avoid another predicted wind increase and hit the cut around lunchtime. The worry was how to calculate how long it would take for us to reach Apalachicola after taking the cut and then the river, also named Apalachicola.

There was no one to ask. But for Captain's Cove, a marina with a handful of slips at the entrance to the cut and a few bass boats, we were never within speaking distance of another person. The only two sailboats actually in the cut were in ruins, lashed up to pilings missing their walkways and tied together, holding each other up in order to keep from drowning. They almost seemed like scalped heads placed there to warn us about what dangers lay ahead.

The cut was the same industrial, man-made canal that exists all over the world, inhabited by broken down barges, occasional businesses both operational or abandoned and left to rot, high bluffs, and scrubby vegetation made so by the elements or the paper companies' extraction of the better trees. Its depth was perfect, wide enough for two barges to pass, and there were no impediments to navigation. Therefore, as predictable and dull to the eye as it was, it was still comforting. Nothing truly bad could happen to us in the cut.

It was the river beyond the cut that stoked my fears. The meandering curves, strong currents, dark waters with cypress tree limbs dangling moss over the water's edge, and flotsam of limbs and logs: they were all more ominous than I expected, and as the sun began to lower in the afternoon sky they became more so. As is the case with most great Southern rivers, its dangers enhanced its wonder, and there was a picture worth taking in every view.

Eagles and ospreys flew over the banks of towering cypress trees, their knees clinging to the edge like an old-time baptismal procession, their canopies fading into a blackness just beyond the river's edge. Disjointed clouds, white on top and a pale gray on their bottom, hung low and heavy just above the tree line, their yellow-orange edges portending the day's end. It was a painter's dream in the winter—but I wondered about who, other than us, would share the light.

There was no marine traffic other than a few small bass boats, seemingly all of them containing two people bundled up in puffy coats from head to toe, their tiny exposed faces like carnival dolls with bodies so large that they appeared cartoonish as they watched us pass by. They weren't given to talking much even if they were close enough to do so.

The only warning given to us before entering the river was to "beware" of Lake Wimlico—"beware," not the less-worrisome "be careful." It was a five-mile passage across a large lake that the river flows into and then exits. The lake is unremarkable in the winter, surrounded only by gray trees, but probably a fisherman's dream in summer. The guidebook warned that it had a narrow channel with five sets of channel markers one mile apart. To depart from the channel at all was to go aground in one- to two-foot waters, way too shallow for our keel.

By the time we reached the lake we realized that sunken and abandoned house boats were the norm on the river, none of them containing signs of human life. Even so, I saw it as another bad omen that the last green fishing house before we entered the lake had been ripped from its moorings by currents, floods, or storms, and left dejected on its side jammed up against the tree line, windows broken.

At about the same time as we passed this sad little house, a light fog set in on the dark waters of the lake. It was as if we had entered some low-grade horror movie. It was almost three, and sunset would be around five. We both knew it would be hard to arrive at our destination by dark.

Jay refused to play my game of pretending that we were further along than we were. It would have made me feel better if he had told me that we were closer to our destination, especially since I couldn't see the chart plotter above the wheel. I wouldn't know if he was misleading me. It would have been kinder, but he refused to sugar-coat our situation.

Stubbornly, like it was some badge of honor, he did as he always did, which is give a "glass half empty" assessment on the boat. Chances were good that we would still be blindly navigating the river's curves after sunset, and in lots of danger, as there were no safe anchorages and plenty of dredging operations closer to our destination, not to mention the rushing current against us. The only good news was that the alligators and snakes were asleep for the winter. I hoped.

Did I really need to know the ways we might die in the cold water? The odds in its favor? And just why was I on a boat with a captain who had to be always giving unvarnished truths?

I'm not sure that we ever made a trip with the children when they were little without some "we're going to die" moment, usually involving the one-cylinder Volvo engine on the Cheoy Lee stopping in the middle of a rushing channel under the Dauphin Island bridge, barges in sight ahead. Each time it was a bonding experience (if you pay for it, it's called "team building")—the "all for one and one for all" pep talk.

Our children, along with their cousins and friends, were really great team players, which I believe is why they are such wonderful adults today. Still, I'm not foolish enough to think they'd let us take their own children in a 27-foot sailboat with a malfunctioning engine across Mobile Bay. That's not to say that they wouldn't do it and do it extremely well—they just wouldn't let us do it. Children have long memories.

While Jay counted down the minutes until dark and the miles to go, temperatures were dropping and clouds appearing on the horizon. Concern morphed into full-blown anxiety (for me, at least) when, in the middle of Wimlico lake, with no signs of life other than clumps of vegetation floating past our keel, the engine unexpectedly but decidedly raced.

It only happened for a brief moment, but our hearts stopped. Then it went back to normal.

My first inclination was to look for places where we might get protection for the night out of the path of a wayward barge, if any arrived, and that were safe enough for the boat. It wasn't a good situation. Nothing fit the bill, and calling anyone for transmission advice was a lost cause—we had no reception on our phones. It was way too early for a mayday on VHF, although I thought I saw a few buzzards circling the boat.

Mentally I ticked down the list of reasons of what might cause an erratic transmission—maybe a fuel filter—but anything I could envision we had taken care of sometime earlier. Jay had the same mental process and result. The logical question, then, was not if the transmission was dying, but when and where its demise would occur.

The fact that I am writing this is a testament to the fact that it did not die, nor did it race again that day. Incredibly, it happened again in the same lake at almost the same place (beware of Lake Wimlico!) on a later trip, and one or two random times in the Gulf for no reason. Each time, after it misbehaved and captured our attention, it would run better than ever to please us, like a child who has done something wrong and suddenly decides to rake the yard.

But I didn't know how it would end on that late afternoon with nightfall creeping up on us. There was nothing for me for to do on the remainder of the trip other than, quite literally, breathe. It helped. We pulled out the jib for the bit of assistance that the wind direction gave to us and proceeded on, trying to quell the apprehension of what lie ahead like the first explorers in those lands must have done.

Chapter Ten

No one likes to see a dredge, especially in a light fog without any idea what it is doing and whether we should pass it on the starboard or port side, but it was our first sign of life and meant that someone might help us if needed. The problem was that the barge was in the middle of the river, and it was impossible to glean any directional information from the dredge line configuration.

Unfortunately, all of the workers had already left for the day. No one answered the VHF. There were no occupied homes on shore.

Without any signal as to the correct choice we took the boat to the port side, risking the 50-50 odds. This time we both held our breath— but we were correct.

Once past the dredge, I became hopeful. Houses emerged on the riverbanks that were not floating upside down or stuck in trees, and they had signs of life within them. Even better, with people and cellular coverage, we were able to contact the marina in Apalachicola—one specifically chosen from a waterway guide because it was still intact and had electricity, heat, shower, laundry…you name it. I had been dreaming about it since Pensacola.

Right after dusk when there was still a small sliver of light, I threw the dock lines to the owner of the marina at the downtown Ice House. A sense of release came over me. It was a perfect landing for the three-boat marina: the only operational marina with power in town.

I hadn't had a shower in over three days. I had almost no clean clothes. And I was ready to rejoin civilization.

"We don't have showers."

What? No long hot shower?

"How about laundry?"

"Nope, all gone."

I was quiet, thinking about what amenity was left.

"Internet?" I barely whispered.

He shook his head.

I smiled as best I could and said, "no problem," because sailors aren't whiners, and griping about hurricane damage is heresy. I'd survive. At least our cellphones finally had signals. The children were glad to hear from us but were never worried. I wasn't sure what to think about that—how many days would I have to hold on to a cypress tree limb dangling in the cold river before anyone wondered about us? But then I laughed. That's the sailor in them—never overly reactionary.

The thing about the *Gypsy Lady* is that she can do almost anything with power, and the Ice House marina did at least have power. The minute our 50-amp cord was connected to the new white power stand on the dock, the heater came on full blast and we turned up the music. Happy hour was ready to begin. I enjoyed a brief, hot shower on-board and took out the one set of cleanish clothes I had saved for that night. For style points, I roughed it without my sock/gloves on my hands.

We hit the streets of the perfect little fishing village like sailors on payday. Apalachicola looked very much like it has for the past hundred years. Although the marinas and buildings on the water's edge were damaged in the hurricane, the city center was thriving.

It was a Thursday night, and we didn't know the lay of the land. At first all we could see were people everywhere without masks hanging outside bars. Eventually, we would find it was a half-and-half city: half COVID responsible and half "live and let die."

We had been too careful to mess up this late in the game, so we wandered around peeking into restaurants for a safe spot to land until we saw the soft lights of the Franklin Inn, a two-story hotel originally built in 1907 and meticulously restored. It beckoned to us just as it has drawn in other seafarers for a century, the flame of the candle on an empty table next to the window signalling warmth and safety. It was only six and we would be dining alone in the large first floor room with its white wood walls, safe from the crowds. Time was irrelevant to us. Only sunrise and sunset mattered, the sun had set, and we were pumped.

Maybe the word should be "jacked." With chapped cheeks from the cold and wind, sun-bleached hair, and our Helly Hansen jackets, we felt like winners. It hadn't been an Olympic sail, and wasn't something other sailors don't do all the time, but that particular week I knew that we were two of the few sailors fearless enough to head out into the open Gulf in January—at least without a lot of compensation. That sense of accomplishment coursed through our veins.

Dinner was like a journey back in time. Not only could we have been sailors from a hundred years ago on shore leave in the best inn in town, but we felt like the younger versions of ourselves that I feared were long lost. It wasn't only the incredible food of local oysters and shrimp and a foreign bottle of wine at a candle-lit table by a window—it was me looking at Jay. This man who wore suits every day suddenly wore his sailing jackets much better.

The vibrancy that I recalled in him from the cold winter GORC races so long ago had come back. The fire was still there—it just needed stoking.

And me? For way too many years I had been a mother, then first mate, then fourth mate as the boys grew older, until finally everyone else took on the mate roles and I became just the person to pay the bills, stock the boat, and take a trip now and then.

But then there was COVID, and there was no one to be mate but me. It wasn't that I was the first or fourth mate—it was that a second set of hands was often essential. If I didn't go, *Gypsy Lady* didn't either. Despite all my insecurities on January 3rd, I stepped up to the plate and took a swing. It was only then that I knew I could do much more.

Since leaving Biloxi we only spent a few nights in a slip, long hard days of sailing in cold weather and into unknown ports. Finally, I felt that the *Gypsy Lady* was mine—there was no part of her that I hadn't explored. All the things that periodically stressed me out on a random day of sailing were quieted by the rhythm of anchoring, docking, fueling, and sailing. They had once again become second nature.

More than anything, I found that *Gypsy Lady* fit me just like Jay and I fit each other. That too-deep cabinet and box refrigerator? I'm not sure if I grew taller, but I definitely grew more agile. Somehow over the five days nothing was too deep and out of my reach. And the large salon windows—they always had pretty views at eye level once under sail. I called a truce with the dreaded full-length mirror that all my friends agreed added at least ten pounds of extra weight. It was no longer my nemesis, but instead my personal motivator.

We stayed at the marina in Apalachicola for three days in order to wait out the strong winter front that was slowly making its way across the region. During that time we ate our way through the town's best food, always at outside tables with heaters, the whole experience so European in service and so quintessential old Florida in flavor. We ate way too many oysters, cooked local shrimp on the boat, devoured Cuban sandwiches and breakfasts, and even found homemade bread for sale from a local restaurant. For three days we admired the city's architecture and explored its history, and I bought warm gloves and hats.

As cold as it was, it was ironic to learn that it was in Apalachicola that Dr. John Gorrie invented what is now known as air conditioning in an effort to reduce the impact of malaria. The museum, with the original mechanical cooling machine was, of course, closed due to COVID.

But all good things must come to an end, and when the wind died, we moved on to Carrabelle, about thirty miles east and our next stop on our trip to the Bahamas. Our refrigerator, which we didn't really need in January, had a glitch and we were assured that the small town at the mouth of the Carrabelle River with a good marina had the best mechanics on the coast.

Chapter Eleven

E verything changed in Carrabelle.

It wasn't that the refrigerator mechanic couldn't fix anything or that the town had the feel of an outpost in the Old West. It changed because of two e-mails we received.

First, in a momentary victory of man versus on-line appointment horrors, we finally secured vaccine appointments at home, and second, our European sailing friends received confirmation that they were included in the Atlantic Rally for Cruisers (ARC). They would be racing across the Atlantic Ocean in late fall and invited us to join them, as well as to sail across the Mediterranean in the summer in a preparatory trip. Both the summer trip and the Atlantic Crossing would be on the brand new 46-foot catamaran that they had just purchased.

The desire to continue our trip to the Bahamas was there—we had a perfect weather window to cross to Tampa that week—but in less than ten seconds we made our decision to turn back.

We blasted out e-mails to our family and friends in Pensacola. We were headed home. No Bahamas this year.

Actually getting home for the vaccine was a logistical nightmare, especially due to the short time before our appointment. We didn't have time to motor, much less sail against the wind, back home. Our first thought was to rent a car in Carrabelle and drive home, get the vaccine, and return to Carrabelle, perhaps continuing on with our trip to Key West, even if not to the Bahamas. That might have worked if Carrabelle had a car rental agency or drivers of any kind, which it didn't.

Over the course of our trip, we discovered that all those things we had taken for granted or just expected to exist in the great state of Florida were not there in Franklin or Gulf County. Right when we believed Florida was the center of the universe, with things like spaceships, cruise-ships, and Disney World, we discovered real signs of civilization were nowhere to be found. No Uber or Lyft in Carrabelle or Apalachicola, or even Port St. Joe (except supposedly one guy late at night). Forget Avis and Hertz.

I'm not complaining that the towns haven't been infiltrated by those mega-corporations. I love the isolated places in northwest Florida and the serenity of Wakulla Springs, cypress-laden rivers, and the white sand dunes of the barrier islands. We savored true Florida, untouched and unfiltered, like bourbon straight up. At the same time, it's good to remember that such experiences are not without their limitations.

We began to go west, back the way we came on *Gypsy Lady*, with only a few minor modifications. One was that, due to bad weather, we planned to stay at Captain's Cove in Port St. Joe after leaving Apalachicola, rather than completing the long run to Panama City without a break.

Late afternoon the next day, we slipped back into Apalachicola after an easy sail along the beach. This time we had been advised to tie up at the city dock since we wouldn't need power and were only staying overnight. But once there we were stymied.

The sign read: No docking. Fee required. You must call the Police Chief.

I groaned.

The Police Chief was the notorious public official who never returned my numerous calls about a slip in the town harbor on the first leg. Apparently, he was not only in charge of the police and the city harbor, but he oversaw the city docks as well. I'm all for rules and fees, but I also knew that he probably had my number blocked from the dozen calls I had made the week before that he never answered.

It was after five and I didn't know how to contact him. I decided that I'd been ghosted enough by this man. Jay and I looked at each other, shrugged, tied up to the dock, and went out to eat another incredible meal.

We left at sunrise, motoring through the river, this time with the current, and passed through the cut to Captain's Cove outside Port St. Joe. We had made arrangements to stay in a lay-up slip with a few other boats. There was nothing close to the marina other than a very tall bridge that we intended to sail under the next morning.

Port St. Joe is the kind of small, eclectic, historical town that romance authors love, with a tough past and romantic future. It was created by the enormous paper company with the same name: from 1938-1999 the St. Joe paper company methodically removed the trees from the region and then spewed out the smells of the paper-making process into the Panhandle air. Ultimately, the paper plant shut down. By then land development had become a more lucrative way to generate income.

As it had already done and would continue to do on this trip, our lack of local knowledge resulted in hilarious experiences. I wanted a pizza for dinner and to buy some groceries. We hitched a ride with someone from the marina, but because of his frequent hacking and his smoke-filled car we thought it might be safer, from a Covid perspective, if we walked back to the boat.

Remember that bridge that went up so high as to allow our boat to easily pass underneath? Well, it wasn't so easy to hike across town with bags of groceries in strong winds, and once we made it to the bridge, we navigated the tiniest sidewalk tucked down one side of the roadway, most of it sixty feet above the water. The hike was worsened by speeding trucks and cars whizzing by while we tried to hug the concrete railings. I was worried—it was only a matter of time until we were hit, hurled over the side of the bridge, and landed on the deck of *Gypsy Lady* far below us. Splat!

When I was about to sit down and scream in frustration at everything from hurricanes to not having Uber, a white truck suddenly stopped beside us, all four windows open, and a man about our age at the wheel yelled for us to hurry and get in. Momentary hesitation hit me, but for fear of a collision, we followed his direction.

"Headed to Captain's Cove?" he asked us once we began to move, glancing in the rear view mirror to examine our stunned expressions in the back seat.

We nodded yes, too shocked to say anything—reminiscent of Key West.

"Thought so. I saw the sailing jackets."

I exhaled. It turned out that he had already received his vaccines and was in town fishing. Still, he pointed out with a hearty laugh, he was being cautious and had opened the windows before he stopped for us, and he felt pretty sure his wife would be mad if she knew he had someone in the truck.

The owner of the large fishing boat beside us at Captain's Cove, he was one of those men that you instinctively can tell is good, and by the end of the night he was one of our new best friends. We were collecting them along the Gulf Coast like fine diamonds. In fact, he did the rarest of things—he gave us premium fish he had caught that day and cleaned. No one, no one, gives up fish they've already cleaned—they only give them away because they don't want to clean them.

The next morning, at daylight, we left for Panama City only to find out that all the furious weather fronts that had passed over us for the past weeks had been channelled into large swells coming in from the Gulf, now running side-ways to the boat. It was hours of the most uncomfortable cold weather, riding the waves, being slammed broadsides by random super-swells, and relying upon our engine while the wind was on our nose. Sailors are a superstitious lot and it only made sense to me that the water gods were punishing me for not contacting the mythical police chief, a.k.a. dock master in Apalachicola, and paying the mysterious dock fee.

In Panama City we were fortunate to be able to stay in a restored modern marina in the city proper. Although it was without its main harbor, the city was still a vibrant tourist, boating, and military community with enough marinas that welcomed a transient boat like *Gypsy Lady*. And it had power. It was going-out-to-eat vacation time once more.

Best of all, we could rent a car from the Toyota dealership to return home for our vaccines in two days. From there, friends and family were close enough to hop on and off the boat and sail as they wished until *Gypsy Lady* was safely back in her slip. We welcomed the company. Sailing alone was energizing, but sailing with others was entertaining.

All in all, the trip to Carabelle and back took six weeks, much of it re-tracing our steps back home. By then it was late February; the days were longer and the weather milder.

Chapter Twelve

O ur six-week summer trip to Croatia and Italy to learn the mechanics of our friend's new boat was scheduled to begin in mid-June and last until early August. I planned to be home in the states well in advance of the due dates for the births of my two granddaughters, one to each of my son's wives. They were expected to reveal themselves at the end of August.

Jay planned to leave in late September or early October, depending on the weather, in order to board the boat in Gibraltar. He and two new crew members would help the owners sail the boat to the Canary Islands in plenty of time for the start of our first Atlantic crossing. Once at Gran Canaria, they would leave Jay on the boat for several weeks while they flew home.

This tentative plan meant that we only had a little over three months after the conclusion of our Florida sailing trip before flying to Croatia to learn the ropes on the new catamaran. It was a great summer vacation boat, and we hoped it would also be perfect for the trip across the Atlantic at the end of the year. It certainly was roomier.

Gypsy Lady is only 12 feet wide, while the beam of the catamaran was over twice that, at 26 feet. That extra width gave the manufacturer the ability to fit in four virtually equal staterooms, each with a full-size bed and storage underneath, and each with its own head with standing shower—two on the starboard side and two on the port. An owner's edition has only two staterooms on one side and a large one on the other, but that is seen as less favorable. Boats with four staterooms are more easily re-sold for use as charter boats. Finally, there were two small berths in the forward section, one in each pontoon, for a captain and first mate to occupy on a charter.

The area between the two sets of staterooms contained the galley, a table with bench seating, and a separate captain's station. The center room between the four staterooms was functional, but not really meant for lounging except in very bad weather. All along the walls of the staterooms and in the salon, there were closets, drawers, and cabinets, as well as covered storage holds in the floor.

The covered aft-cockpit, where most of the daily activities on a catamaran occurred—including eating—was located at the stern of the boat. It was about 200 square feet on the new catamaran, most of it filled with two long lounge seats and a table with two fixed benches. The cockpit sides were filled with built-in ice chests, outside refrigerators, and other compartments that took up much of the actual floor space.

Based upon our prior experience, I knew that when we were not in our respective staterooms, six adults would share a space about the size of a large master bedroom.

In the summer when we sailed the Adriatic on catamarans, the forward cockpit had lounging cushions and netting between the pontoons, like a trampoline, that provided extra seating and space. However, for obvious reasons we wouldn't be sunning on cushions on the bow during the November crossing. Finally, the helm above had a reclining cushion area behind the skipper's bench seat.

Even a new boat requires a lot of preparation for an Atlantic crossing, especially one built primarily for pleasure, like the catamaran we would be sailing. Not only did the owners want to make many upgrades to the boat, such as solar panels, but Jay and I were responsible for making sure that all of our personal safety gear, fishing gear, and other items necessary for the Atlantic crossing would be ready that summer when we flew to Croatia for the test run. Given COVID and shipping delays, there wouldn't be enough duffel bags or time to prepare between our summer sail ending in August and when Jay returned to the boat in late September. Therefore, we decided to buy and bring all of our equipment and other items requested by the owner on the June trip, and leave them on the boat until we returned in the fall.

I knew the preparation drill because we had prepared the *Gypsy Lady* to sail in the Pensacola, Florida, to Isla Mujeres, Mexico, race in 2020. The race was ultimately cancelled due to COVID, but not before we already added thousands of dollars in required electronics and safety items to our boat. We dropped fees across the Gulf for every imaginable permit and insurance upgrade. It was incredibly time-consuming, especially when ordering specialty items and unusual parts, because everything is a special order when dealing with a Hinckley. I felt like it would be much the same on this boat.

The owner paid for all expenses associated with the operation of the catamaran, and they were not insignificant. For everything else, especially provisioning, we paid our proportional share and more. I knew there were items that made life easier on a boat, so I also bought things that I felt were absolutely needed, such as non-skid dinnerware, insulated glasses marked with the crew member's names, a pasta pot, a vacuum sealer and bags, plastic baskets, a stove-top coffee pot, and more, while Jay bought top quality off-shore fishing gear and anything he could think of to make the boat more enjoyable. The more we could help the better.

I didn't know much about the ARC at that time and had a lot to learn, from registering as crew on an international voyage, to our other responsibilities as members of the rally, to the ARC in general.

The World Cruising Club, with offices at Isle of Wight, United Kingdom, has been coordinating an Atlantic crossing rally since 1986, attracting boats from around the world. It hosts two regattas—the ARC (Atlantic Rally for Cruisers) and the ARC Plus, in which we would participate. The ARC's route goes from Gran Canaria in the Canary Islands straight to the island of Saint Lucia in the Caribbean. The ARC Plus route would take us from Gran Canaria, down the coast of Africa to Cabo Verde, and then across the Atlantic to Grenada. The only year it did not run was in 2020, due to COVID.

The World Cruising Club has a set regimen of preparation for ARC participants. We, the crew, began our required training in the winter months. On each Saturday morning, even while still on the *Gypsy Lady* on our way home, we would painstakingly convert our local time to that of our instructors in England or wherever they might be located, then try to remember to stop whatever we were doing and log on to the website at the random starting times, often confusingly set on the half-hour.

There were classes on a multitude of subjects that all crew members were expected to know, including safety, communications, navigation, weather forecasting and patterns, sails, and first aid. Many classes had videos we were to watch before the live classes began on Saturday mornings. We dutifully watched them all. It helped that it was COVID time and we had nothing better to do than watch sailing videos, dream of leaving our homes for the seas, and follow up by ordering off-shore life vests with personal locator beacons and other expensive gear that ARC-Plus required, in addition to the rugged off-shore fishing gear that we wanted.

Of course, once we started ordering sailing gear off the Internet, pop-up ads began to appear everywhere, enticing us to BUY MORE, BUY MORE. I had no idea that there was so much pretty, pricey, and enticing sailing paraphernalia that would make our lives better. By the time we left for Croatia, we owned more SPF-50 clothing and hats than we could wear in a lifetime and had contributed more than our share to the uptick in the economic forecast that month.

Overall, the classes were worth attending. It was fun to interact with sailors from around the world. Stories of past trips whetted our enthusiasm each week and more than once the class taught us something new and potentially critical in case we landed in the wrong set of circumstances.

One of the more important suggestions we were all to follow, according to the instructors, was for the whole crew to spend several weeks together and evaluate everyone's skills before the race. In other words, verify that the crew members were as skilled as they claimed to be (or were teachable) and ensure that you would get along well enough to spend over a month at sea together in very close quarters without use of a washing machine. In the end, the instructors emphasized, we would have to all know how to do everything on the sailboat, but I knew our roles would be defined by what we were best at.

This was especially true on the catamaran. Shortly after we committed to the trip, the owner had asked us to help him find two more people to sail on the crossing, preferably a couple, one of whom knew how to dock a large boat. It was not an easy task.

The conundrum that new yacht owners find themselves in is that most of the time they cannot operate the vessel alone, so either family, guests, or paid crew are needed. There's another option as well—if you include human trafficking.

This meant that I saw lots of million-dollar yachts bought solely for this passage across the Atlantic, usually to fulfill some bucket-list item, with owners that had probably never sailed alone or even commanded a boat, so it was mandatory that they hire a fully seasoned crew. Other boats I saw only needed a captain or other crew member who had crossing experience.

Potential paid crew applicants usually post their names and resumes on websites, include references and ratings, and list reliable expectations—especially what their role will be on the boat. They will request foods they like and can consume easily, preferred watches, satellite phone times, proper life vests and safety equipment, airfare, insurance, and any other items that they can negotiate. It sounds good, but let there be no mistake, once they are hired the owners and their captains are perfectly entitled to treat the crew as paid employees and instruct them to do almost anything they wish. At the same time, they do so at their own peril. The crew members are also usually free to quit and go home.

Chapter Thirteen

*B*y the time we started our search and I took a quick look at the crew-for-hire list, it appeared that many of the quality paid crew members were already taken by other boats. I knew that Jay and I were as competent or more so than most of those that remained. We thought it would be nice for the owners to have a young adult or two to go up the mast and help with the sails, but Jay could climb the mast and the owner preferred another couple with a man to handle the docking, so it was a couple we sought.

All of our friends either had responsibilities or no interest in a crossing. Some told us they had been there, done that, and were not interested in doing it again. We next looked out into the broader sailing community and recalled a couple that we thought might fit the bill—sailors with professed skills we had met at a yacht club dinner. The husband had been a work-boat captain and was a sailor. He was also a diver who could check the props and rudders with a mask and snorkel. Both the owners and the two new crew members were slightly younger than Jay and I—instead of saving for grandchildren's college funds, they were seeing their youngest finish their educations. In the scheme of things, that was not much of an age difference. It might work.

Other than those basics, Jay and I didn't know much more about them except that they were amiable over a cocktail, and after some Zoom calls with the owners, the owner asked them to join us.

They wouldn't be paid crew, just as Jay and I weren't. Loosely, we might have been considered guests, but in the real world of yachting, guests are waited on by the paid crew. When there is no paid crew, however, everything changes.

We were the guests/unpaid crew, the type of passenger who is in a state of fluid expectations, one day toasting champagne with the owner and the next day scrubbing the decks when some errant crumbs are found. Guests who are invited because of their skills add another level of complication to the equation. They bring their own equipment, and they also buy for the good of the boat—not just food and wine, but fishing equipment, cooking supplies, and anything else they see that might make life aboard safer and better. They split the provisioning bills and other costs, plus pay all of their own airfare and travel. It's not cheap, but it's doable.

Guests/unpaid crew may act like paid crew and look like them, but their mindsets aren't the same. Unless they are seasoned sailors, guests don't normally ascend the mast or pull down a stuck mainsail on someone else's boat in the middle of a hellacious squall. They aren't required to understand the boat's systems, whether they are mechanical or electrical, or to become truly responsible for anything—but they are usually happy to learn. They don't sign contracts or agreements, or make promises that they don't want to keep. I have heard someone say that the boat and its toys may be the owner's circus and animals, but guests aren't aboard to clean up the cages.

Both the other couple and Jay and I considered ourselves invited guests, who happened to be sailors and were willing to be unpaid crew. What that actually meant was to be determined.

Our upcoming summer weeks in the Adriatic would offer a perfect opportunity to see if the crew of six—the owner and his wife, the other couple, and Jay and I—would coalesce, and for us to get familiar with the new catamaran. The owner planned an Adriatic overnight crossing and chances to sail toward, not away from, strong winds until we were all comfortable with reefing the mainsail and making sail changes.

There was no reason for me to worry about whether everyone knew the basics of sailing. Two were captains, two were the owners of the boat we would be taking across the Atlantic, and the other wife was supposedly working on her captain's license. They all were very confident in their abilities.

I might have been confident with my forty years of sailing experience, but given the self-proclaimed heavy-hitters at the top of the very short roster, I wasn't about to oversell my skills.

As a result, I agreed to be the medic on board. Now, I've never been a nurse or done any work in the medical field—and I hate the sight of blood—but I am the daughter of a nurse, and my daughter-in-law Melanie is an ER nurse. Unfortunately for my medical training, my mother not only had a full-time career but also four children. All I gleaned from her about medical care was: "Take two aspirin and go to school." I'd need a lot of Red Cross classes.

Nevertheless, my qualifications were apparently enough for me to be chosen to save everyone's life.

I embraced the role and eagerly watched the ARC expert during our "medical" training session. After a long time spent trying to sell an expensive list of recommended medical supplies for an ocean crossing, the training became a bit confusing when the German doctor hosting the on-line seminar began to repeatedly refer to a "coroner" as the "corona." One might ask why that would matter so much, but it turned out that most of the participants from around the world were inordinately concerned about what to do with the body of a dead crew member, and this worry consumed all of the Q-and-A period. It wasn't reassuring to me as a first-time participant, but at least I learned that I should call, not drink, the closest "corona" upon seeing a dead body.

Despite the occasional stifled laughter of the participants, the seriousness of the German doctor in the medical session got my attention and I spent months perfecting my "Nurse Betty" role. I hoped that after all the first aid classes, tutorials by ER nurses, practicing stitching, and reading captain's medical books that I knew as much about handling a live body as a dead one, but I wasn't sure. There are hundreds, if not thousands, of ways you can get injured and die on a boat.

My son told me that the most common injuries are shoulder and back injuries, the kind where someone pulls or strains a muscle and then can't do anything but lay around. They don't really look hurt, however, so slowly the remainder of the crew, stuck doing the injured person's chores, begins to suspect malingering. I thus intended to let the crew know the dangers of becoming flotsam on a ship, and that they should work hard to avoid soft tissue injuries. That is how Boat Nurse Betty operated.

It is a truism that the best way to be healthy on a boat is to arrive healthy. When boaters began asking about what to do with chronic illnesses, the ARC-Plus moderator candidly told them that if you have a serious underlying illness this probably is not the trip for you. It made sense to me. The boat owners and other crew members were slightly younger than Jay and I, but we were in excellent health and had recent physicals.

Other than the medical updates and shots, the other component of healthy sailing is physical agility. After a year of no gym and COVID eating and drinking indulgences, my agility was still mostly limited to lifting a glass in my right hand. I decided that in order for me to get fit quickly and not get injured in a fall off a Bosu ball, I needed to swim. The only problem was that I wasn't a good swimmer.

I first learned to swim via the "throw your sister in and see if she drowns" technique. That means that for my entire life I perceived myself to be a strong swimmer, while the truth is that I most resembled those poor children on the movie Jaws, who were last seen flailing in the water while the drumbeat of the movie's theme song reverberated across the theater. I was older now and determined not to be the last crew member in line swimming away from a killer shark. So, to the natatorium I went.

My goal was to be able to complete one mile in laps before I left for the Adriatic. It would give me confidence not to panic if I were dumped into the water for a spell, and I would be able to judge whether I could swim to shore if the boat became disabled. I also wanted to at least look like I knew how to swim when I would be surrounded by women who looked like models that could be on any state swim team.

The first day I barely made 25 meters. Maybe I started out too fast— surely, I could swim more than that. I began to worry when I tried the second 25. I wondered if the lifeguards really would see me drowning if I had a heart attack. I was in the deep end, after all, and they didn't appear interested. I wondered if anyone had ever quit after 25 meters before, and how embarrassing it would be. After I struggled to do several more laps, I pretended to do some stretches and headed home in humiliation.

I didn't quit. For the next two weeks I floundered around in the city pool until I could swim seven or eight laps. I felt enormously proud of myself until I asked the surly lifeguard how many times across the pool equated a mile.

"Seventy."

Surely, he was in jest. I couldn't swim ten lengths, much less keep track of counting to seventy.

Luckily, his smug response made me mad, but not enough to quit. I was motivated. I bought a lap watch. I watched videos on proper breathing and arm techniques. I read articles on the best mix of strokes and regime for my goals, and I kept on swimming two to three times a week. At the end of the second month, I was able to swim a mile in less than an hour. It had seemed like an impossible feat in the beginning, but I had done it. I pumped my fist in the air like an Olympic winner and asked the lifeguards to ring a bell (they didn't).

The next month I started slowly shaving off the minutes that it took to swim a mile—along with inches off my waist—until it was time to leave. I had done everything possible for a healthy voyage, and it was time to go.

By then the natatorium was fully operational, bright sun streaming through its open steel-rimmed roof panels. Spring was in full bloom, and COVID was in the rear-view mirror. We were vaccinated and life held nothing but potential.

Chapter Fourteen

S till, there was one hurdle left to clear: my mind. Just like a novice atop the platform of a high dive, I wondered if in October I would really hurl myself out of my comfort zone…if I would throw my bags on board and sail over 3000 nautical miles across the unpredictable Atlantic as a tiny speck in a sea full of dangers.

The problem was this: it would be awful of me to spend the six weeks on vacation learning the boat only to bail out when the time came to actually leave the Canary Islands and cross the Atlantic. Not just awful, but shameful, leaving Jay alone and the boat one crew member short a month before the trip. Either I decided for sure I was taking it all the way—summer in the Adriatic and winter in the Atlantic—or I didn't start at all.

No matter how many clothes I bought for the adventure or idyllic island times I envisioned, there was no way to block out the images of disabled boats and medical emergencies I was taught to avoid, not to mention the library of books and movies about the sea that existed in my mind. Forget the four Jaws films, it was the true terrors about murder at sea like The Sea Will Tell and all the "trip gone bad" movies like Adrift, or Robert Redford's "All is Lost." Horror spun in my mind like the reels on a projector, subliminally reminding me that there is a reason they never have a movie about sailing without a near-death experience. "Listen, listen to my tale of woe…"

It's not like I had to go. I didn't have a bad life I wanted to escape. There was no marital discord or financial disaster or warrant out for my arrest. Something like that would have propelled me across the sea in a second. A crossing also definitely wasn't on any of my bucket lists.

Both Jay and I knew the October trip was perfectly timed. How long would we remain healthy and situated so perfectly for a trip like this? Life is fragile and, in a minute, could unravel. Should I go with Jay and embrace the risk or live with the knowledge that I chickened out? Or should I be grateful for the safe life I already possessed, with family and friends, instead of striving to be someone else, another me, one that I didn't know or even recognize?

Pride never let me express any doubt in public, but it must have been there, hidden behind the smile plastered across my face later when lists were prepared and plans for every meal and minute laid out by the other two women on board—with little input from me. Not because I didn't have thoughts and opinions, but because that was the way it was.

"Are you sure you're going?" someone would look up and ask me, to which I would smile and answer, "that's my plan."

Only I knew just how tenuous my departure was becoming as I realized just what it would be like for months on end with no escape. The summer pre-ARC six-week trip wouldn't only test the crew's ability to get along. It would also include a fight between my mind and heart— whether to romantically pretend that I am still twenty-three and can take anything that is dished out by man or by sea, or remember that I have already proven myself in life and career, and acknowledge that sailing across an ocean wouldn't change my legacy.

Even I know that I can't change the hands of the clock by sailing backwards across the time zones.

What would I do in the end?

"I don't know. It's a mystery," said the actor playing the part of Phillip Henslowe, the owner and manager of the Rose Theatre in the 1998 movie, Shakespeare in Love. It was his answer after he was asked how to proceed when confronted with "insurmountable obstacles on the road to imminent disaster" in a theatre production.

Once I took the plane to Croatia, I intended to be in it for the long haul. But intending is not doing. What would occur between summer and October was still shrouded in mystery, but most likely it would come down to one thing. Just like in Key West decades earlier, I wanted to cross the Atlantic because my husband was going, and because my friends asked me to go. Forty years later and I wasn't sure I had learned anything about good decision-making.

Writers and travelers are mesmerized alike by the knowing of their destination.

Eudora Welty

Part Two
Split to Venice Trip

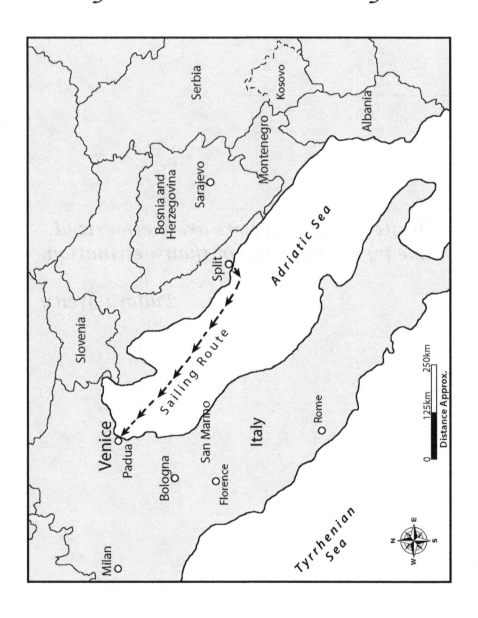

Chapter Fifteen

O ur plane landed on the almost vacant tarmac of the Dubrovnik airport with a tour group of pilgrims, young and old, united only by their quest for some greater meaning to life. There were older women in groups of two, dressed in practical clothes and sturdy shoes, pulling their equally practical carry-on luggage as they peered at their fellow companions through eyes bleary from long days of travel. There were middle-aged Spanish women in groups of three or more, and an American mom, three children in tow—a Bible verse printed on her olive-green t-shirt and a gold cross necklace hanging around her neck.

All of these women had one thing in common: a need to visit Medagoria—a religious site in Bosnia, some 45 miles from Dubrovnik. Each one had a divine belief that their answer or cure lay somewhere over the steep and barren mountain ridge that separated Croatia and Serbia. They had traveled a long distance at a precious price, and cautiously expected a miracle, while remaining stoically prepared to rationalize any disappointment.

I wanted to tell them that they wouldn't be disappointed—miracle or not. The American children would escape their bubble, the older women would be made younger by completing something many desire but few do, and the Spanish friends would grow closer in the midst of unexpected joy, all generating memories for a lifetime.

It was a good thing the pilgrims were on the plane, as we would find out that despite Croatia's affirmations to the world that they were open for business, the sun was shining, the water crystal clear and warming—there were not many takers. Mostly Americans were at the airport, a stark departure from years past, and I learned that they were not renting sailboats.

While our plane was filled with interesting people, it was not filled with our luggage. We landed in Croatia on time, but nothing else did—most notably the three bags filled with everything we needed for six months, including the previously mentioned off-shore life vests and a medical kit worthy of a first-class trauma center. It was nothing we would need or ordinarily buy for the states, but critical to our trip.

"No worries," the airport officials said. It would be here by nightfall. And it was, delivered straight to our boat slip by an earnest delivery man in the waning daylight before a strawberry moon appeared in the sky. It helped that I had written our names and phone numbers in big black sharpie on the red duffel bags and took pictures before we departed.

Our catamaran was the only boat tethered to the shiny stainless-steel bollards at the end of a covered concrete pier over a hundred feet long.

The lack of occupancy by other boats and people at the five-star Marina Frappa, boasting showers and bathrooms that would outshine a Ritz-Carlton spa, was our first exposure to the struggle the marine industry was suffering in the time of COVID. The still waters around it were only agitated by the occasional enormous blue Jardolinas that ferried locals and tourists from island to island. The few mega-yachts never left the slip. The only visible movement on them was the crew members in matching shirts polishing windows, hulls, and railings.

We weren't planning on a long stay there, and less than twenty-four hours after landing in Dubrovnik we released the dock lines in the marina. On board were the owners, the wife's sister, and Jay and me. According to our plan, the first two weeks would include sailing with the owner's sister, the next four would incorporate the two other crew members joining us on the crossing, and the last few days we would spend with other members of the owner's family. It would all be training time for Jay and me, but vacation as well. We were free to leave the boat in ports, shop, and sightsee, but we also intended to take the time to really understand the catamaran and help in its operation.

We knew the owner's extended family and were happy and content to spend days with them sailing, swimming, shopping, and playing cards. On the other hand, the couple who would join us for the crossing was still an unopened envelope. What looks good on paper may not be so good on water, and Jay and I were anxious to see how they would acclimate in a European setting on a catamaran in moorings they had never before encountered. A lot depended on how they would act under stress, especially docking, which was the main reason the owner wanted them aboard.

We'd have to wait for two weeks until they flew into Split. Before then, for the first two weeks, we were tourists.

Vacation time began with a sail toward Mljet State Park, on an island with the same name off the coast of Croatia almost mid-way between Dubrovnik and Split. Like most of the trip, we alternated motoring and sailing as the winds allowed.

At any given hour, sailing between the thousand Croatian islands is like navigating a narrow fjord with rocky barren land on either side, or peaceful sight-seeing in a calm river lined by stone houses with red tiles roofs and marble wharfs. But it was easy to feel small and vulnerable in large open expanses of the Adriatic, interrupted by tiny islands topped with lighthouses that often resembled cruise ships in the distance. Our first day of sailing was an example of the latter, with winds that enabled us to unfurl the jib and glide across small waves unbroken by land masses.

The favorable winds meant that by mid-afternoon we were back near land and had the boat anchored in a protected cove off Mljet. A few hours later we frolicked like kids in the natural salt water lazy river created by tidal forces around and within the island. It was our second visit to Mljet, the other time made five years before on our first summer charter with the owners. This time, unlike before when the captain docked on shore, we chose to anchor out, dinghy to land, and take a taxi to the lakes. We then ferried to the site of a Benedictine monastery built in the 12th century on the small St. Marie Island, an island within an island.

The boat waited patiently for our return from its anchorage in the most protected bay in the Adriatic—at least according to the Romans whose palace ruins still sit in the middle of the small town.

Unlike our first experience, when we arrived at Mljet this time we encountered far fewer visitors, and most were Croatian families. None were Americans. The only similarity between our first and second trip was that on both occasions we succumbed to the attraction of the walk downhill through the small farms and vineyards to the shoreline. No one remembered until it was too late that the several kilometer hike was actually—quite oddly—all uphill. Only at the bitter end did it slope steeply downward to the cove and our tethered dinghy at the dock, a perfect place to take a quick dip and cool our blistered feet.

Later that day, while sitting with my face toward the afternoon sun, I reflected that in less than twenty-four hours we had sailed, swam, hiked many kilometers, eaten ripe tomato salads, and feasted upon fresh fish that we caught that afternoon. My morning began with the European ritual of cappuccinos and croissants, not to be confused with the afternoon ritual of espressos and a tall glass of cool sparkling water. In the late afternoon I sipped on local white wine. It was so easy to fall back into the structured but relaxed life of Eastern Europe.

The familiar ritual of island hopping and favored stops, the circuitous laps around the Adriatic designed for optimal sightseeing amidst time constraints were perfected by charter companies in order to make money. I assumed that things would be different this time with less movement and more long stays because the owners could take the catamaran wherever and whenever they wanted, but that was not the case. Whether you chartered or owned, almost all boats followed the same well-worn paths—the island loops and stops were mostly the same, charter or not. There were just more of them. Boats are always on the move, but to the same places, seeing the same boats around you, eating at the same favored restaurants. Each time we stopped, however, it was a unique experience, digging deeper into Croatia's way of life.

Chapter Sixteen

*T*he early morning sun of day two washed the cove in yellow, and the water's surface was a black mirror reflecting the bright white hulls of the few boats anchored there. My previous day's introspections were behind me, and we were pulling up anchor, ready to move and ruffle the water's surface. The boat's itinerary was the owners' alone to decide. Vaccine cards in hand and safety masks on face, I was ready to go along.

The quiet of that morning portended a day of yoga-like bliss, lounging alternatively in the sun and shade. But just as we were lulled into napping, clouds suddenly appeared and the sky grew gray, with enough wind that we could sail.

We hoisted the new Code Zero, a large light air sail primarily deployed to take maximum advantage of light wind. Sometimes it was used along with a small jib and other times alone. The downwind or reaching Code Zero was the primary sail we would use on the trip across the Atlantic. We practiced using it under conditions that mimicked those we would encounter on the crossing, or so we thought.

That day also marked the beginning of my six-week familiarization with the buttons and levers that were used to operate the sails, engines, and all other moving parts of the boat. Modern catamarans have all transitioned to computers and electric winches to pull in the lines. There was no "hoisting the sail" anymore—it was pushing the red button, or one of a number of others at the helm.

The helm of a new catamaran is a command center that operates almost all the moving parts of the boat, with a half-dozen screens that display endless amounts of data about all of those parts. It has an autopilot that is almost always engaged, an enormous wheel that hands don't touch, and a self-tacking jib that requires no thought or effort.

The helmsman is more like an engineer at the Kennedy Space Center in Cape Canaveral than an astronaut soaring through space. There is no feeling the wind in the sails, the torrents of water rushing past the rudder, or the power of the boat. Everything is mechanical—all handled by and dependent upon instruments and the settings the owner preferred. It was a techies' dream boat.

I quickly realized that Modern Multihull Sailing 101 was a late in life education that I would learn, may only use once, and quickly forget— much like a six-month French immersion language school. But, like I would need to know how to ask for directions for a road trip in rural France, I also needed to be familiar with the function of each button on the boat. It was necessary information upon which our lives might one day depend, and by the end of the trip I must know the boat's systems.

The fact that I was only now learning them should have scared everyone, but the fact was it was new to everyone else as well.

On *Gypsy Lady*, there are only a few important items that need artificial brains to work, mostly the navigation system or complicated mechanical or electronic components. The boat may not have a roller-furling main with mechanical reef points, but Jay and I know from experience that we can handle anything our trusty main sail throws at us even in the worst of situations. It will never be stuck inside a mast like an unreachable broken piece of elastic in a waistband. Our main sail may fail, but when it does it will be out in the open for all to see—no hidden surprises.

First-time boat owners, like our owners, must quickly learn all the critical nuances of sailing that even the best sailors might only gather over the course of a lifetime. It's a task that, despite all the confidence in the world, is impossible to do well in a hurry. As has been said before, you can't have enough replacement parts for everything on board— you must accumulate the parts to re-build things that break. That takes a lot of knowing.

In the worst-case scenario owners choose, or are forced to choose, what is most important to know—usually the basics—and when bombarded with too much information, make a conscious decision to "not know what they don't know." Some perks of the boat are so complicated that they are rarely or never used. Owners often rely upon complex gauges, not realizing the failure rate in them, much less the gaps in the information they give.

In the end, sailing is all about intuition gained from experience. That takes time and is often learned from mistakes made along the way.

The next day re-enforced my strong opinion that trips to foreign countries shouldn't be all about fancy restaurants and expensive wines, top-ten destinations, or even cultural sites. Foreign experiences are about dropping anchor in a protected cove with a former German submarine cave and seeing women with Bond-girl physiques swim a hundred meters with heavy dock lines in their hands to a slimy, sea urchin infested shoreline, only to climb up a jagged rock wall to tie the stern dock lines to a tree or rock, while their spouse yells directions to them from the boat, engines running. Everything could go wrong, but somehow it doesn't.

That operation is called a Med mooring, and according to some, it is the best spectator sport in Croatia.

Incredibly, what went wrong occurred during a simple dinghy trip to the market. We didn't go with our hosts, but were relaxing in the cockpit when they returned from their errand, silently admonishing us to stay quiet. They were accompanied by two surly police officers on a 20-foot wooden boat containing a small square office from which to write tickets. These men were serious and nasty—the dinghy had momentarily exceeded five miles per hour and the offense was the biggest crime in town. In a matter of minutes, the happy sounds from people in the bay were gone. Fellow boaters, swimmers, paddle-boarders, and especially the big yachters, disappeared into their boats. Even the men who pick up mooring fees by boat turned the other way, choosing to come back later. It was like a drug bust in a college dorm.

It was a very expensive fine—almost $200.00 US—but they wanted to add more charges, if they could. It helped that our owner had all his registration and entry forms on hand, but I have to hand it to the police for perseverance. They kept fishing for other possible misdeeds for an hour or more before they gave up.

I was set to blame it all on pretty little Lastovo Island, where we were—close to Italy and at one time occupied by Axis forces from Germany and Italy, and later the Communists—but then I found out the police were from another island, Korcula, and had been trolling Lastovo for fines all day. We were the eighth catch for them, and another catch came after us. I imagine it was a good day in police world. I thought about it later when we went to Korcula; given the downturn in the economy, I decided they probably needed the money more than we did.

The summer trip coincided with Jay's and my fortieth anniversary. We spent it at the Hotel Solitudo, an older, sprawling hotel that sat high upon a rocky knoll in the small town of Pasadur on Lastovo Island. Pasadur is located where two inviting bays meet, and the hotel occupies one side the inlet of water that fills and empties in a strong tidal action extending to the nearby hills. Both banks are cinched by a small stone bridge, the water rushing under it toward the lagoon where our boat lay. On the other side of the tiny bridge were homes with purple bougainvillea vines and shady trees, pots over-flowing with flowers lining stone steps that climbed up a seemingly endless maze of homes, all overlooking local swimming areas and lots of local life.

Based only on the rumor that Conde Naste recently recommended the Hotel Solitudo (the name says it all), we reserved a room for the night. It was a three-star hotel, usually great in Eastern Europe, but we found that it was quickly slipping to a 2-star status. Sadly, we were told by locals with their heads dropped in shame, it was now run by Russians. But even the lack of upkeep and the spotty air conditioning couldn't diminish the views, or dent our anniversary experience.

The only real problem was that we found it impossible not to occasionally glance at the brand-new catamaran that would be our second home for several months that year. She sat peacefully in the lagoon across the water. When we did succumb to the urge to see if she was still there (as if they would actually leave us), we would longingly look at the boat's stern where our stateroom was located, feeling as if we'd been exiled to the hotel like Napoleon was to the Isle of Elba, and without any Croatian Kuna, or working ATM, or in-room coffee.

It made sense that the next morning we were dockside an hour early, ready for the owner to pick us up in the dinghy. We were much like expectant children waiting to be picked up from a week at camp; glad we did it, but happy to be headed home. We didn't exceed the five mile per hour speed limit on the way back for even a second.

Chapter Seventeen

*F*rom Lastovo, we sailed and sometimes motored to Korcula, its old round city rich in history and architecture, built like a fine pewter ring topped by circles of jewels with an ancient steeple in the middle. For centuries it was known for its strategic location in the Adriatic.

Although Korcula is famous around the world for many things, including its connection with Marco Polo, on the particularly sunny Sunday afternoon that we were there the fame didn't include tourists. Locals told me they were counting on the Americans to come. I saw five. All of the Marco Polo shops in Korcula were closed.

That was painful to me. I love Marco Polo's life story. The best way to experience how life was for Marco Polo in the 13th century is to visit the Croatian island of Korcula in November, when the cold winds from the Dinaric Alps blew across the narrow strait of sea separating the ancient city-island from its motherland.

Marco Polo was born in 1254, probably in Korcula, and was from a Venetian noble family. His father and uncle (Niccolo and Maffeo) were merchants trading with the Far East along the Spice Road. When Marco Polo was a young lad, the older men took him along on a lengthy trading trip to China where he had all of the adventures one would expect on such a journey across the globe in the 1200s.

But for the fact that sometime after his return from China Marco was captured at sea, we wouldn't know much about him. By then, he was forty-four years old. It was while in prison that Marco fortuitously met Rustichello of Pisa, another prisoner who happened to be a romance writer. I didn't even know they had romance writers in the 1200s. Given a lot of time and nothing else to do, Marco told Rustichello exciting and spell-binding stories about his time on the Spice Trail and in China with Kublai Khan. Rustichello knew a good story when he heard it.

With plenty of uninterrupted time to write, Rustichello became the ghost-writer for Marco Polo, and put his fascinating stories on paper in his romance-style writing as opposed to the technical writing of the time. It was a good move. The manuscript known today as The Travels of Marco Polo was an immediate success and at the top of whatever the equivalent of the best seller list was at the time in Europe. It stayed there for a long time. Two centuries later Christopher Columbus read it, enticing him to leave Spain and heave-ho to China, admittedly making a slight miscalculation in distance and direction.

After the story was published Marco became a celebrity, hit the talking circuit, married a Venetian patrician's daughter, and had three daughters of his own. It sounds a lot like the successful authors of today.

But fame often courts controversy, and as fate would have it, poor Marco was to be wrapped up in controversy the rest of his life. Cynics could not wait to crawl out of the woodwork and ruin a good story, and they did it with a venom that matches the worst of today's tabloids and book critics. Surely, they opined, this little man didn't do any of those things.

To be clear, I'm a Marco Polo believer. As a travel writer I know that when I return home from an extraordinary trip, my family and friends listen to my stories up to a point—but eventually they've heard enough. The same is true for most people, and definitely was true for Marco. The exciting travels and success of his book were too much, and it made him a target for those men in very hot Venetian suits with puffy sleeves and lots of velvet who wanted to suck all joy out of someone else's travel to an exotic location, especially when they were home working.

It is said that even on his deathbed his family and friends brought the priest in and begged Marco to retract his stories. But Marco Polo, my hero, is said to have risen from his deathbed and said this to them: "I have not told half of what I saw." No one would believe him. I say that should be considered one of the most famous quotes of all time. Considering the fact that centuries later his book is still widely read today, he has a popular Netflix series, and a great pool party name, it only makes sense that I would be enamored with his life.

As a result of the financial distress brought on by the lack of tourists in Korcula due to COVID, along with the fact that the Marco Polo shops were closed, I bought a swimsuit cover-up that I didn't need, a cute top I have nothing to go with, postcards without addresses to send them, pistachio ice cream (again, I didn't need), wine, and local sea salt with herbs. Even as I paid, I knew my purchases were but a pittance to the "cash only" entrepreneurs. There was a sweetness and sadness to them, a resignation that we could only buy so much. I wanted to scream to my fellow Americans, "you wanted Europe to open up to you and Croatia did so at great risk during COVID and they all have vaccines and masks—why aren't you here?"

Three hours north of Korcula is the island of Hvar, the "hotspot" of the Adriatic, and our next stop. There are three equally charming but different main towns on the island, Hvar City being one of them. Only it was not such a "hotspot" when we arrived. The ancient city's edge hugs the water and marinas, where we jumped out of our water taxi. We quickly searched for shade on the hot day and explored the interior part of the city, which was anchored in the middle by a large square and the Cathedral of St. Stephan built in the 14th century. It was uncharacteristically quiet, with only the sounds of the local children as they swam, rode their bicycles, or laughed as they walked past us in small groups.

As the day grew long, the sounds of children were overtaken by the animated voices of adults, all dressed in red and white checkered jerseys ready to cheer on the Croatian World Cup team at one of the outside restaurants and bars that lined the perimeter of the main square and harbor. Croatia played Spain at six that night. Croatia lost, which was very sad to me, but then the Croatians clapped for Spain at its overtime conclusion for a job well done. Our waiter (the owner's son) even gave free Limoncellos to the five Spanish girls reveling in their victory because, he said "they were too pretty to ask to leave." I wasn't so sure anyone expected Croatia to win. It had been that kind of a year.

What Hvar City lacked in people it made up for in super-yachts. While Americans missed the memo, owners of yachts from around the world turned on their engines or hoisted their sails to find the harbors of Hvar, where size is no limit. Some charter yachts anchored empty as they waited for tourists to eventually show up. Others, with small numbers of guests, primarily Europeans, pulled alongside each other, rafting out from the seawall.

In all my travels I've never seen so many huge, sleek yachts in one place. They were different in design, but the same in amenities.

Most had small pools tightly fitted on a top deck, which often looked like the contraptions my brother and I would create as children in order to enjoy a "pool" experience. They all had an oval dining table with seating on the stern's aft deck, like our catamaran did, which assured the guests that they could see and be seen, but without much canvas they offered limited protection from cold or rain. Narrow decks, or no decks at all along the sides, assured there would be more space for ample staterooms below. Small windows in creative designs along the waterline allowed a modicum of light into the spaces where the kitchen and crew worked and lived. Finally, massive space-age electronics perched high above the flybridge in rounded containers like a bird house stand full of over-sized buzzards…or some criminal operation in a James Bond movie.

Often the only difference between the yachts was whether the owner embraced the dark look and went all black and gray, chose the classic Jackie Onassis white and wood, or ignored any style at all and went solely for big. The biggest ones also added a helicopter pad to their decks—not exactly a stylish addition, but definitely showy. Their matching tenders cost more than my house.

The weird thing about the big yachts is that I almost never saw anyone on them. Privacy is the name of the game.

By Hvar City my "mega and super yacht-envy" stage of life was pretty much extinguished. I love yachts and would hate a world without them, but a three-hundred-foot yacht is really a cruise ship in disguise and only meant for show.

There was nothing lacking in comfort on the catamaran we were on except a lot of crew members in uniforms waiting upon us. Neither the catamaran nor our *Gypsy Lady* needed a big screen TV or more sunning decks than they already had, and certainly no pool or 20-foot bar with a water-fall wall. Cocktail hour was no less divine on our boat than on a boat ten times the size.

The only boat I really wanted to buy was the water-taxi that took us to Hvar Town that night. I had expected a white wooden boat with hard seats and gunnels so low on the side that waves and wakes would drench us. But Hvar had changed over the years. The Colnago 33-foot luxury speed boat, with a turquoise hull and bright yellow over-sized cushioned seats, classic teak decks, and 420 HP Cummins inboard engine, our chariot to and from the catamaran, was a different experience. Its massive engines sped across the water in the dark of night at close to 40 mph. The plumes of frothy white wake that crested behind our stern were higher than most racing boats and were made more dramatic and mesmerizing by the light of the full moon above.

All I could think of was how much my father and brothers would have enjoyed the ride.

Chapter Eighteen

We finished week one in Stari Grad, also on the island of Hvar, a much quieter and more understated locale. It is the oldest city in Croatia and one of the oldest in Europe, with a deepwater cove in its center lined on either side by hundreds of small fishing boats and a smaller amount of pleasure boats and yachts. I had visited it before but never explored all the hidden back alleys, businesses, and residences.

The ancient city center was deceptive—it looked small and compact, with the traditional tourist enterprises and restaurants lining the waterways, but once I strolled a few steps away from the water, narrow roads emerged, fanning out like spokes on a wheel toward enclaves of picture-postcard homes, small courtyards, interesting entrepreneurial businesses, and romantic cafés set among historic churches and buildings.

Stari Grad was inviting because it was livable, young, and vibrant. The boats lining the harbor in the city were small working boats, averaging twenty-feet in size, brightly painted, and owned by ordinary fishermen from Croatia, much like they would use at my home. The streets around the harbor felt like neighborhoods, not museums or tourist destinations. It was welcoming and unpretentious. If I had only had an hour to spend on a short shore visit from a cruise ship, I'd never know it.

Still, as inviting as the city was, we really were tourists and because we had a first-time visitor aboard the catamaran, our hosts arranged a mid-day island tour out of the hot sun and in an air-conditioned minivan. The guide was a handsome Croatian of about forty. He and his ancestors had lived on the island for four hundred years.

The trip began by veering away from the docks and city and continued along a steep climb to the top of the large rocky cliffs that rise above Stari Grad. Situated mid-island, it allows for a water view from opposite directions. The guide navigated up its single lane roads, stopping periodically for an occasional passing car or to allow us to take in panoramic views of Hvar and the surrounding islands—unobstructed views that made me feel as if I were above the ground itself, like a bird looking down from above.

Then we turned downhill, into the interior of the island where small ancient villages clung to existence. We gazed upon once-loved stone homes either vacant or now occupied by just a few hearty souls, and wondered how families could leave behind a life that appeared so idyllic. It turns out that those interior villages, strategically tucked into the wooded mountainside and hidden from centuries of marauders, were "done in," not by invading forces but by vineyard funguses, fires that ravaged the lavender fields, over-fishing, and a multitude of political miscalculations.

Now those on Hvar primarily depend on tourism. The rock walls that crisscross the landscape denoting the locations of past vineyards and lavender fields now contain only a few sturdy olive trees or brush. It worried me that just like when Croatia relied entirely upon vineyards, or fishing, or lilac, it now relies upon tourism. The beautiful islands do not offer much of a Plan B for when things go wrong—and COVID was one of those things gone wrong. It was July and there still weren't many tourists. It was the water and the harbors that would lure them back.

I was offered information on the tour that I already knew: that Croatians began to exit their island a century ago when their livelihood did. My hometown of Biloxi sits on the edge of the open water like Stari Grad, and thrives upon the hard work of Croatians who immigrated early in the last century to fish our abundant waters in a climate not so different from their own. Their large Catholic families thrived in an accepting culture over the past century, and now they don't only own fisheries, but they occupy high places in every facet of life, including running the town as mayor.

Our guide was a bit tired that day. His tour was one of the only ones I took in Croatia that high-lighted the other side of life there—tilling the soil as opposed to life dependent upon the water. He had been up since four a.m. harvesting potatoes on his family's farm. The next harvests would be olives and grapes. On other days, when the opportunity arose, he led "adventure bike tours" up the 45-degree slopes to the top of the island and then back down to Stari Grad. He told us it was a gift that day to leisurely drive through his beloved countryside with interested tourists in air conditioning and enjoy tasting his family's wine in the cool of their tiny, ancient wine cellar.

The wine was rich and full of flavor, but I almost cried when he proudly served us pusharatas, a sweet Croatian pastry with nuts, fruit, and rum, coated in a sugary glaze. The small round cookies look a bit like fruit cake but aren't—they have a distinct taste of their own.

Almost all locals in Biloxi have a little Croatian in them, and I'm no different. Suddenly, I had found the very same treat my grandmother made for my wedding and that we gave as gifts every year at Christmas. They are hard to pronounce and spell, but cooks know that they are even harder to make. Apparently last year our hostess made a stir when she mistakenly put too much rum in the batch that she served to the local children. Being from Biloxi I wasn't so sure it was a mistake.

Last but not least, we visited the tiny city of Vorbeska, with its ancient narrow canal cut through the middle of town, a picturesque scene punctuated by arched stone bridges connecting narrow streets on either side. It is appropriately nicknamed "Little Venice."

After leaving the island of Hvar we sailed to another of my favorite stops, the island of Vis. We happened upon the large and safe harbor on a day when there were no charter boats at anchor—it was at the end of a "charter week," and the boats exited early in order to timely return passengers to Split and other marinas from wherever they departed. I felt embarrassingly smug as I waved good-bye to the last of the boat parade while we dropped anchor outside the mooring area.

There were hundreds of floating orange mooring balls spaced out in the harbor along Vis's water's edge, but only one sailboat was tethered to a mooring, a thousand feet away from us. Just as we began happy hour, an erstwhile harbor marine patrolman insisted that we pull up and move our anchor fifty meters further into the bay in order to make sure we kept a proper distance.

"It is the rules," he said. Ah, bureaucracies!

It had been a great vacation week of fair winds and pistachio ice cream, fabulous meals in local restaurants, happy hour music, and lots of card games. And just like that we would be on our way to drop off the owner's sister in Trogir and then to Split in order to pick up the new couple who would join us on the crossing.

We were happy and there was no reason to argue, so we complied and moved the boat. We were even happier when the maneuver turned out to place the catamaran in the middle of the City of Vis's free Internet service.

We left Vis for Split so that the owner could have some warranty work completed before the new couple's arrival. Jay assisted the owner on a multitude of chores, not the least of which was taking the boat to the historic city of Trogir. The mast had to be taken down for repairs and re-stepped. It was a miserably hot three days on concrete docks, but a very interesting learning experience, especially in a quaint town that had more sailboats than cars.

In order to repair a conduit contained within the mast, the boom had to be removed. Technicians detached the electronics, and we moved the boat from Split north to Trogir for the manufacturer's authorized employees to correct the problem. Once the mast was standing again, we accompanied the owner to return the boat to Split, where a different crews performed the remainder of the warranty work. Each step required a professional in that field. It was all done in three days—just three days. It was like ripping a band-aid off.

On any Friday or Saturday in Split and other Croatian coastal towns hundreds of mechanics and other boat maintenance specialists, not to mention even more boat cleaning crews, descend on the marinas to prepare them for the next departing charters. Split can have hundreds of boats departing on charters on any given Saturday. During the week they handle all the bigger jobs like the mast repairs. There is always some competent person (who happens to also speak English) to do anything you possibly need, and who will arrive on time, with a smile on their face. If you have an appointment at noon for a re-routing of cables, you can rest assured that the right person will be there at noon, dressed in clean work clothes, with all the tools needed to accomplish that purpose.

Even the commercial docking wasn't really an issue, because several men were there with the correct fenders to ensure that our boat haul-out was seamless. They didn't expect the owner to do anything.

I think that is one of the reasons that so many boats go unused in the states. We haven't managed to create a desire for young people to become marine maintenance specialists by treating them as professionals. We don't make it enjoyable, and we don't teach it in school. Without professionals to lend a hand, weary boat owners become frustrated and abandon upkeep, which ultimately leads to their boat's demise.

It is one of the reasons that we enjoy interacting with boat owners who are active sailors and work to keep their boats in good repair, especially those who do it by their own wits. Not only are their adventures often amazing, but they also have a wealth of knowledge about repairs, problem solving, and upkeep, in addition to navigation advice. Half the time they will hop on your boat and show you how to do something. There is an intellectual and mechanical side of sailing that, when a problem is conquered, can prove just as satisfying as a perfectly trimmed sail. And, as part of the sailing community, Jay and I want to ensure that our boat can always pass an inspection and offer proof of seaworthiness, rather than joining the ever-growing population of abandoned or derelict boats that give sailing a bad name.

Chapter Nineteen

*T*he two new crew members for the Atlantic crossing arrived in Split right on time, their taxi dropping them off on a narrow road high above the marina parking lot, half of their luggage with them and half somewhere between the states and Split. Even from a distance, I couldn't miss them with their rolling duffel bags and mix of American and European sailing clothes. The wife was very slim, like the owner's wife and a bit taller than me, while her husband was about her height with a stockier build. They were as light-complexioned as the owners were dark-eyed and brunette.

It was only when they came closer that I saw the look of exhaustion and frustration on their faces due to a long flight during COVID, plus lost luggage. I correctly worried that it would cloud their ability to see the beauty of the late afternoon sunlight on the water.

By the time we went to dinner, their aggravation about the missing luggage continued unabated. I told them that I had learned from experience that eventually it would arrive, and it did. Until the moment when the missing bag hit the boat, though, they spent an inordinate amount of time on iPads and making calls, which only made them more frustrated.

It is hard for an American to do, but I was anxious for them to try to think more like Europeans and just roll with the punches. I saw the subtle signs and watched the news, both portending that it would be only days before Split exploded with thousands of tourists from an open EU. They would be sorry they missed any of Split on an iPad while they could be wandering empty streets.

Their lost luggage may have upset them, but it didn't dent Jay's and my excitement about their arrival. We had such high expectations. The owner was even more excited, as he would no longer be at the helm when the catamaran pulled into a fuel dock. It was all good.

Both Jay and I knew that Jay could, and has, handled an even larger catamaran, not to mention a larger trimaran with only one engine, plus once co-owned a 45-foot powerboat with twin engines. Most of the time the wind practically docks a large boat by itself, but the new owner and his wife were still learning the docking process and Jay had little incentive to risk inflicting the first ding in the gelcoat of a new boat, especially when the new crew member said he was an expert.

In fairness, he modestly explained that putting a work boat up against an oil rig with tires all over the sides required no particular expertise. Nevertheless, his confidence was enough to calm the owner.

We only stayed one full day in Split with the new couple, eating pizza on the marble seawall, gazing at the beautiful boats everywhere, and later touring Diocletian's Palace. I wanted to stay a month.

Split is the "mother-ship" of docks and marinas for cruisers and charterers in the Adriatic. If you are a sailor, this is the city to know, and that has been true for thousands of years. There are more than two thousand chartered boats in the summer in Croatia, and most of them depart from Split. A large, ancient city on an enormous natural protected cove, Split is the one city I would move to in a foreign country. It is not only beautiful, but it is modern enough to provide every comfort for a long and full life.

The actual city center has remained for over two thousand years in one square mile of land that began as Diocletian's Palace. Century after century the citizens built and rebuilt on top of the remains, leaving mazes of narrow winding streets of polished stone and occasional open squares where churches tower over nearby homes and businesses. Still surrounded by walls on all sides, the city gates, Gold, Silver, Bronze, and Iron, open up to the sea, the green hills to the west, or the business areas to the north and south.

It is shocking to the mind to walk a few feet out of the ancient palace through the Silver Gate and be met with the luxury of modern yachts, cruise ships, open air restaurants, and blue waters beckoning you out to sea.

Diocletian built the palace in the early 300s when he became the first Roman emperor to retire alive from the position. The emperor, his wife and daughter, and the palace's history are too fascinating and important to serve as a mere back-story in any book, much less mine. It is best to learn about it for yourself by staying in one of the tiny apartments in the Old City for a week and wandering about until you become part of the past. Visitors who saunter off a cruise ship for a few hours only scratch the surface of the history that lies between those walls and beneath its floors.

Split wasn't the only old Roman city we would visit on our way to Venice. The owner planned to sail north into unfamiliar territories for me, away from the Dalmatian coastline and toward the Istrian coastline, including stops in Porcec, the Kornati Islands, Rovinj, and Pula. Our last stop would allow for the Croatian border patrol to document our exit. We intended to depart Croatia before reaching Slovenia in order to cross to Venice.

Sometimes hopping from city to city in the Adriatic on a sailboat becomes a blur of names you can't pronounce and places that all sound alike, but they aren't alike. I admittedly have trouble pronouncing names. It's frustrating because often sailing is about reaching destinations, and no one likes to forget them quickly.

Croatia can be like that sometimes, but certainly not when it comes to the Kornati Islands and Pula. The islands were only reachable by boat, which limited access to most tourists. Pula, on the other hand, while accessible by land and with a deep and protected harbor, was far from the normal sailing circuit, which limited the charter business. To access either place by water was special.

After we left Split, we sailed north in their direction, stopping at smaller protected coves next to small cities such as Porcec, a precious town with a stone church towering atop the high hill marking the center of the island and city central. Porcec's sprawling graveyard spilled down around the church like a topping on a sundae. In the late afternoon when we arrived, the church doors, were open and the exiting weekend worshippers stopped with us to watch the sunset splash across the horizon beyond the city. It was worth the steep climb up. Once back to sea level, we were rewarded with a local street festival.

Sure, all of that could happen in any European city, but on that summer day in that place, we were the only Americans there.

Chapter Twenty

S hortly after we left Split, a city filled with hospitals and pharmacies, we had a medical emergency, and it came with a big lesson. Although crew members are asked about potential medical needs, sometimes people don't tell someone they barely know all the prescriptions they take—whether because they feel like they have it under control or simply don't want to divulge it to others. This can present a problem without a real doctor on board.

The emergency came during the day in Croatia, but unfortunately it was in the middle of the night in the states. The husband of the other couple reported his wife was suddenly rendered very ill from a medical issue that had flared up for which she had forgotten her medicine from home. The woman didn't need a prescription for typical medicines in Europe, however, she needed one for her particular highly-regulated medicine in Croatia. Just to add icing to the cake, her husband insisted that absolutely nothing else worked. It wasn't just a medical emergency—it was a mess.

The captain spent hours in the first city we approached, Rovinji, attempting to get the medicine for her, going from one pharmacy to another until he was able to perfect a pitch. He was eventually able to obtain one dose for that night. The next morning a prescription had been emailed from the doctor and the matter was ultimately resolved, but by then it had been a very stressful twenty-four hours.

All the time they were away on land Jay and I dutifully stayed on the boat, which was at anchor in an almost empty cove in a building wind. It was not a great place to leave the boat unattended.

When the four returned for the final time, the weather had worsened to the point that we could no longer stay at anchor where we were. This caused a chain of events that unfortunately meant we abruptly left the city and missed our opportunity for a nearby tour of Tito's infamous Zoo. More personally, it meant that Jay and I missed our only opportunity to visit the city of Rovinji, a city more Italian than Croatian, one of the prettiest towns on the Istrian peninsular, and a favorite of travelers across Europe, especially Germans. One day, I told Jay, I'll go back.

It was the first time that I had sailed with several other couples in many years. Traveling with other couples is always a trick-bag, and now that the trip was underway, I wondered if it would it all work out with three couples in fairly close quarters. It dawned on me that we didn't see other boats with the same mix of crew. But, then again, I had taken many trips with multiple couples and had a wonderful time. Surely it would all be fine.

Jay said he married me because I never complained on the Key West trip. He certainly misread that one, but the truth is that we love sailing together while other couples sometimes disintegrate. Sailing is not for the spouse who expects to be treated with privilege, unless there is a paid crew somewhere aboard. What they are entitled to, however, is kindness and respect. Jay and I have worked hard to not place blame for mistakes on each other, and even harder not to heap blame on others, even when due. That wasted too much time and energy that could be more productively spent on a solution. I learned long ago that it was the high fives, not the rolled eyes, that made happy sailors.

I had a lot of time to pontificate about life and marriage on the sail through the Kornati islands, a Croatian national preserve. It was almost like the barren islands were there to prepare me for the onslaught of colors, sounds, and romance of Venice.

It was an ethereal passage northward—a perfect aloneness gliding through a mystical place. Even I found no particular reason to talk as we slid past bleached white islands of stone rising above the calm blue waters, bare land but for a few hearty shrubs. It was an eerie grouping of rocks that created an almost vacant archipelago of twenty miles and over one hundred islands. Much of what we see today occurred slowly over the past centuries when pillagers clear-cut what trees were there, until the islands had little purpose other than housing a few goats. Despite this, the waters between them offered lee passages, abundant seafood, and the occasional sight of picturesque pastures. It was as magical as predicted.

George Bernard Shaw once said this about the Kornati islands: "On the last day of Creation, God desired to crown his work, and thus created the Kornati islands out of tears, stars, and breath."

Who am I to try and explain better why it's worth the effort to sail there?

Both the Kornati Islands and the city of Pula near the top of Croatia are destinations sailors dream about, but rarely see. Even before sailing I wanted to see Pula, which has at its city center one of the most intact Roman amphitheaters in the world, along with other architectural wonders, including the ancient Temple of Augustus, believed to have been built during the Emperor's life between 27 BC and AD 14.

The enormous amphitheater was almost empty on that sunny day we arrived. Built by the Romans between 27 BC and AD 68, it's the only remaining arena with all four side towers entirely preserved. It was abandoned for use in the fifth century, leaving the site to be plundered, just as similar sites were plundered across the region. However, unlike the rest of the region, in Pula the plundering ended in the 13th century, when the patriarch at that time stopped wealthy people from Venice from stealing the marble steps and columns as ornamentation for their villas, and the locals from taking the rest.

It was a constant battle for centuries, but progressive thinkers over time were able to preserve the remains, including thwarting an attempt by Venice in 1583 to dismantle the arena and move it to Venice. The last stone to be taken was ceremoniously returned to the city in 1789.

So much was left that it is hard to believe anything of value was taken, but it was and would have continued but for a smart patriarch and those forward-thinking politicians. The arena would be nothing but a barren site in the middle of a port town, sad and empty like the hole left at the top of a spent volcano. Today it is a spectacular venue used for concerts and town events—a work of wonder and a destination that was worth all my pent-up desire, not to mention a photographer's dream. I hated to leave, but Venice awaited.

Chapter Twenty-One

We arrived in the ancient city of Venice a day later in the late afternoon, a stealth entry in the quiet, with no cruise ships, freighters, or other sailboats—just us, navigating a complex and confusing channel full of lights and markers. We sighed with relief as we exited the tight entry channel leading to the quiet marina alongside the marshes just outside the city proper, where we would be staying for the next few days. It was one of those rare moments in travel that actually deserves the adjective "surreal"—entering Venice by sailboat through its canals, as others have done for almost two thousand years.

On the other hand, taking the ferry to find and then clear customs and border patrol across town in order to properly enter Italy, was more mundane and tiresome. By the time we were approved by all authorities to wander Venice, masks in place, it was past time that the three couples part ways for the day and meet at night for dinner.

Almost immediately after the others headed in different directions, Jay and I found ourselves alone, walking in the middle of the main square, Piazza San Marco, usually one of the most crowded spaces on earth in the height of tourist season. No so that day. We took endless pictures from every view, with not one other soul in sight.

For the next two days Jay and I walked miles over narrow arched bridges, visited museums (no lines), and joined the others for the reputedly best pizza in the world, at least according to the owner and Jay. It was romantic, peaceful, and thought-provoking. I bought two Venetian rocks glasses made by Murano, one in blue and gold glass, the other purely in gold, a splurge for later days to remember the trip.

Unbeknownst to us upon arrival, our final evening would fall on the Festival of the Redeemer, and only Italians with their passports were allowed to be in the city. In fact, all of the boat moorings along the Naval Park boardwalk were reserved for the hundreds of Italian boats that would see the fireworks that night.

Early that day we watched families lay out blankets and place on top of them candelabras, fine china, and delicate wine glasses, ready for the evening's fireworks. Pavilions were strung with lights, and music wafted through grassy open spaces. It was a pleasantly warm sunny night. Love and friendship filled the air. All the ingredients of Renoir's Boat Party painting were there.

But the feast wasn't meant for us. It was a personal gift from Venice to itself on the third Sunday of July to celebrate the end of the 1576 plague, which killed 50,000 Venetians. The parallels to all the COVID restrictions were not lost on the Venetians, and we had no intention of being intruders.

The famed fireworks began as we returned to our boat some distance away and continued long after we went to sleep. It was an epic display seen for miles. No red, white, and blue, though—the sky lit up with green, red, and white. I left Venice, as usual, wanting more and dreaming of a civilized life in a small apartment there. I resisted thoughts of sea level rise and flooding like I avoided the thought of hurricanes back home.

We pulled out of the slip in the marina a few days later at daybreak, when a billowing ceiling of dark foreboding gray was layered above benign lower clouds, which were tinged with vivid variations of pink and orange from the rising sun. The dramatic sky confirmed what we knew—that the sail down the coast of Italy would be a difficult one. But then I saw it—a small bright blue hole emerged in the middle of the darkest clouds. The opening was surrounded by bright yellow-orange, darker on top and lighter below.

In that still moment of the morning I saw the tiny bit of cerulean blue sky as weary sailors and painters have for thousands of years—a peaceful reminder that there are indeed heavens above, and perhaps they would be protected by a hand descending below.

Even with the re-assuring break in the clouds, we abandoned plans to sail further down the Italian coastline due to strong headwinds and lack of safe harbor. Instead, the owner said we would sail overnight all the way back down to Vis. He felt the need for the six of us to experience an overnight passage before taking the long Atlantic crossing.

The owner planned for us to sail 220 miles straight to the island of Vis in Croatia and properly enter at the tourist checkpoint there, which is what we did. As expected, we all performed well. However, I did discover that most Adriatic fishing boats don't use navigation lights, much less the AIS, the automatic identification system. They also didn't seem to care about the navigational rules that a sailboat under sail (no engine) had the right of way, so long as the fisherman were not actively engaged in a fishing activity. It was a good reminder that night watches were there for a reason.

The next day we were back on the island of Vis, eating pistachio ice cream cones as we waited for hours in the hot sun to clear customs back into Croatia. After Vis, the owner planned to, and did, return to his familiar and favorite Croatian places, much the same as a charter where the captain moves the boat day by day from island to island, year after year. The only difference was that in our case the owners had been operating their boat for less than one year.

We were still adjusting to the new couple when we left Venice. It's hard to put into words how the closeness of being on a boat together can work on a person—and I am a wordy person. Benjamin Franklin, who crossed the Atlantic about eight times in a sailing vessel, the last being when he was age 79, had a lot to say in his journals about the difficulty of life aboard with the same people for a long period of time.

He was the wittiest of all American heroes, and candid, especially in his journals. This is how he described his shipmates: Our company is in general very unsuitably mixed, to keep up the pleasure and spirit of conversation. Ouch. I wondered if they knew what he thought.

All of the six personalities on our boat were out there in the open by Vis.

The new man was often withdrawn and serious. He had no use for frivolity or those who engaged in it. I assumed that his career and interests didn't leave room for it.

His wife was happier, especially when she was instructing others or cooking.

The owners were much more serious now that they owned a very fine boat. It wasn't playtime as much anymore.

All in all, there was no real problem. The biggest issue I foresaw was that I was beginning to increasingly see signs that the other two couples were more introverted than I had previously considered. I was a card-carrying extrovert and as an extrovert, not only did I want to be happy, but I saw it as my role in life to make sure everyone else had a good time, whether they wanted it or not. Jay was not far behind me. Our joie de vivre was one of the reasons we were on the crossing.

Different personalities can happily co-exist on a boat—they usually add more enjoyment to any occasion, assuming everyone has a little give and take, and some sense of humor. Still, we were all so different, and I'd never been confronted with such a long stay in close quarters with two other couples.

Could we really co-exist happily for almost two months without any escape?

I shook the thoughts out of my head. Despite the ordinary worries a sailor might have about crewmates, personality disputes were not one of Jay's or my big issues in life. The success of our careers depended upon being genial with everyone, as much as being knowledgeable. It'd be fine.

The confidence and bravado that existed forty years ago had not yet fully left me.

Split was not the same scene when we returned from Venice to drop off the new couple, all hugging good-bye. The owners wanted the new couple to take the crossing with us, and we were relieved to not have to look for replacements.

I turned my attention to the two weeks after they left to savor a carefree sail to Kyrka Falls, eating oysters in the salt-making city of Ston, and a refreshing swim in the salty Adriatic twice a day.

At the end of the six weeks Croatia was filled to the brim with tourists. When we finally said our good-byes to the catamaran and headed home, we were hopeful that the crossing would be all that we dreamed it would be. I was as ready as I would ever be.

Hereafter, if you should observe an occasion to give your officers and friends a little more praise than is their due, and confess more fault than you can justly be charged with, you will only become the sooner for it, a great captain.

Benjamin Franklin quote

Part Three
Gibraltar to Grenada
Trip

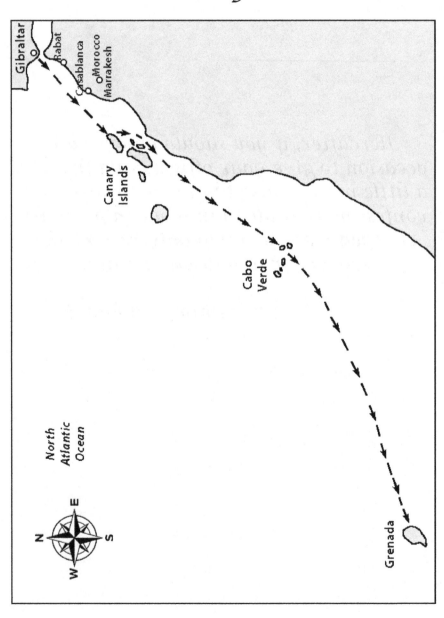

Chapter Twenty-Two

*T*he morning sun was streaming through the weathered six-paned window of the Burger Burger restaurant in downtown Biloxi on September 18th. Fall was finally in the air and the last remnants of Hurricane Ida were gone, leaving in its wake two beautiful baby girl grandchildren that had recently been born to our daughters-in-law. The tropical waves that were forming off Cape Verde, where I would be in a few months, were finally curling north and away from the soon-to-be cooling waters of the Gulf.

My daughter Jennie was joining us for breakfast in Biloxi, a rare treat since she lived in New Orleans. We made reservations for her to spend the week with us in the Canary Islands before we set sail across the Atlantic, and her visit was perfectly timed for finalizing details on flights and an apartment in Las Palmas. We marveled at the cost of the trip—only $400 one-way to Las Palmas, $500 for a modern two-bedroom apartment on the beach for a week, and $45 for Jennie to fly to Barcelona after she wished us bon voyage for the sail across the Atlantic.

The natural highlights in her long curly hair glowed in the sun and her hazel eyes lit up with anticipation for her first overseas trip in many years. As an immigration lawyer for a non-profit over the past six years, she was due a completely frivolous vacation, and I was selfish enough to plan it with me.

Finally, I could feel my enthusiasm for the Atlantic crossing building. Well, at least two of us at the table were excited. For the last few days Jay was uncharacteristically distracted each time I discussed the finances and logistics for his part of the trip, and he gave little input on what we would do on the islands. It was off-putting, but I didn't let it affect my happiness. The departure dates were finally on the horizon.

While Jay had groused for some unknown reason, I merrily plucked travel articles on the Canary Islands and forwarded them to him and Jennie. I ordered two new bathing suits for Grenada. I began to look at water-proof watches. By the time we met for breakfast at Burger Burger I was in full vacation mood.

"Well, we definitely have to climb the volcano," I said, just as the waitress delivered our eggs and grits, hoping to engage Jay. He liked volcanoes and our sailing hosts never missed an opportunity to visit one. "I think it's something like the third tallest in the world."

Jay took a deep breath, put his fork down and slowly turned toward me, staring into my eyes as if checking whether there was a brain behind them. Then he asked, "Do you really not know the news?"

"What news?"

He sighed, slowly pulled his phone from his back pants pocket, scrolled to an article, and began to read aloud the breaking news about the Canary Islands. Obviously, it wasn't fodder for travel websites that I was perusing, much less the bathing suit websites.

According to the article, the week before, on September 11th, seismic monitors detected unusual behavior and underground rumblings in the waters off the Canary Islands. Thousands of times a day in the last week there were small earthquakes, thirty-eight of them passing three on the Richter Scale, their intensity in numbers and size creeping up fast. More worrisome, they began at twenty kilometers below the surface, and they were now at only a few kilometers.

The experts said the earthquakes would soon be felt on land, and they were eerily similar to those that preceded a large eruption in 1971. Las Palma Island was now under a yellow alert. I think they said more, but at some point, I couldn't digest it all.

Just like that, the song "Where do you go when the Volcano blows?" by Jimmy Buffet began playing like background music in my ears.

While I listened to the second-rate and probably off-key version of the song rattling in my mind, Jennie, who is fluent in Spanish, sought out articles from the Canary Island's mother country, Spain, which we thought might be more detailed. Instead, they were less reassuring and less concise. Experts expected something soon, but not today. Maybe tomorrow. Who knows? Maybe an earthquake, maybe just a tourist attraction eruption. More likely a tsunami. They threw out the word "mega" a lot which, I believe transcends all language barriers.

Given that we would be on a sailboat, it was obviously bad news that the Canary Islands were under a mega-tsunami warning. The Spanish news stated that even the city of Neuvo York (NYC) was preparing for the impact across the Atlantic. That made sense, given that the Canary Island earthquake was predicted by some to produce waves up to one hundred meters high—taller than the length of a football field.

Suddenly, the first-floor apartment on the beach in Las Palmas didn't seem like such a great bargain, and the new bathing suits also felt like poor decisions. There wasn't a chance in hell I was going to get on a boat or peacefully sleep at ground level while a monstrous wave might be approaching outside my window, and I definitely wouldn't be sunning on the beach.

I'm not sure I've ever been truly speechless until that moment. This time I didn't interrupt Jay with questions but rather hung on every word like it was a thrilling novel. But it wasn't fiction. When the article ended and Jay closed his phone, I was in such a shock that I couldn't help but laugh. Hysterically. It was either that or cry.

Had I made elaborate plans to leave hurricane alley only to die in a mega-tsunami or be vaporized in oozing magma? We missed out on a sailboat trip from France to Croatia because of COVID the year before, and the year before that our plan to sail *Gypsy Lady* in Regata Al Sol from Pensacola to Isla Mujeres, Mexico, was also cancelled (again, due to COVID).

Now this? With each doomed "trip of a lifetime" I accumulated enough of-shore safety gear to outfit a Coast Guard cutter. The problem is that you can't use that gear for anything else, much less return it, as you have prominently written your name all over it in permanent ink. Now mounds of it sat at home forlornly on my bedroom floor. It was too hard to wrap my head around.

So we all joked. We never uttered the words that we wouldn't go. It was such absurd news that as our coffee turned cold and Jennie continued to read out loud, she kept laughing more and more. This is the same daughter whose wedding was completely decimated by Hurricane Katrina, who wrote elaborate thank-you notes for gifts that were blown away. She definitely inherited my family's appreciation of dark humor.

We all laughed the hardest when she called her brother Patrick on the cellphone to see what he knew. He had taken meteorology and geology in college and was the most likely to have an understanding of the risks. He began by relating what he had discovered, beginning with the words "seismic crisis." I didn't think it possible, but the scientific warnings he found were seriously more troubling than the more general headlines. No one had inserted reassuring press releases from the island's politicians that all was well…kind of…sort of. I think one mayor said it could just be a great tourist attraction.

Eventually, after the plates were removed and the check paid, the laughter subsided, and the weight of the information began to sink in for Jay and me. Did this change everything? How could this be happening? I wanted to scream that it was so unfair, even if deep down inside we all knew how secretly scared I was of taking this trip to begin with.

So, what to do? Jay had been worrying about this issue for two days, which in retrospect I considered a good excuse for his bad mood and lack of excitement about the volcano tour. He said that he had waited to tell me until he had a plan—or the volcano erupted—but I was making way too many suggestions for day trips. Plus, time was slipping by.

In the end we decided to continue to prepare and wait. Either the crack would blow open or subside and go back down to the underworld, like a moray eel slithering back into a crevice. And it if it blew, it was just as likely to happen before we left for the islands, at which time the tsunami warnings would be lifted. In the end, just as it was with the other cancelled trips in the past two years, it would most likely be a decision we didn't make, but rather one that was made for us. Once again, I was afraid that God would be forced to intervene.

Luckily, He did.

One day later, on September 18th at 3:15 p.m., the volcano in the Cumbre Vieja National Park in the south of Las Palma Island erupted, sending jets of lava and a plume of smoke and ash into the air, eliciting joy from volcano junkies around the world and sighs of relief from the island tourism bureau. Unfortunately, it would go on to cause sad destruction on that particular island, but for us on September 18th it meant the crossing was still on.

Maybe, I thought, I really was meant to go. As if to ease my worries, the next day a minister of the Canary Islands said that the islands were safe and the eruption was a great show— "Come to visit." Suddenly my cheap airfare and apartment facing Las Palma Island became hot-ticket items. Briefly everyone, everywhere, knew exactly where the Canary Islands were.

Relieved of the fear that I would actually have to make a decision, I turned my attention back to ordering the new water-proof watch, but at the last minute added "returnability" to the list of its features. I knew better this time. I might buy it, but I wouldn't write my name on the inside of the band in permanent ink until we were past Cape Verde.

Chapter Twenty-Three

*B*oth the ARC and ARC Plus crossings began from the Canary Islands, but first the boats all had to reach the starting location. The optimum weather window for the trip to Gran Canaria ended in mid-October. While many of the boats were sailing south via the coast of Spain and Portugal, an equally large number—including our boat—were sailing to Gran Canaria from Gibraltar.

Since the entire trip would not end until mid-December, sailors who chose this route and timing would be on their boats for more than two months, or even close to three. Many chose to leave Gibraltar in early October while the weather was still nice, and once the boat was in Gran Canaria fly home for two or more weeks. A U-turn flight back to the U.S. after only a ten-day trip wasn't a logical option for Jay and me. There were too many downsides to the inconsistency of air travel, and the COVID situation. Plus, it would be safer for the boat if Jay remained aboard to look after it.

We decided the best option was for me to miss the Gibraltar-to-Gran Canaria leg of the trip, but I would join Jay as soon as I could after he arrived in the Canary Islands. Our two grandbabies were only a month old, over two months was a long time to leave the business responsibilities at home, and the Gibraltar leg of the trip was not expected to be taxing. No one complained because it all made sense.

That one seemingly innocuous decision, to stay home for a mere eight days on the front end of the trip, would come back to haunt me as I was not there to voice my opinion as to critical decisions being made regarding daily life on the crossing.

Jay and the other couple crewing on the boat flew to meet the owners in Gibraltar on October 3rd. Jay and I agreed that he wouldn't use his phone in Gibraltar in order to cut down on the daily international fees. Instead he was to e-mail and text me on the new Apple computer he had bought. Given the money we had already dropped on this trip, it made little sense to be so cheap on the phone charges, except for the fact that cell phones don't work offshore and it was a waste of power.

My biggest mistake was assuming that Jay could find good Internet at the marina in Gibraltar and be able to maintain a line of communication with me from the boat. He couldn't. I incorrectly thought that the satellite phone on the boat was connected for that leg of the trip. It wasn't; a fact I'd only discover too late. That caused our children and me to wonder how would we contact Jay if anything happened at home. Somehow we dropped the ball on communication, a mistake I intended to correct before the crossing.

Jay was in Gibraltar for almost a week before they set sail, and after that he was on the boat for eight days from Gibraltar to the Canary Islands. It turned out that he only had good Internet one time. I only knew when the boat left port by the dots on the tracking service. For eight days I watched a silent blue dot move on almost a straight rhumb line to Gran Canaria along the coast of Morocco. It passed by Tangier and continued by Rabat and Casablanca, ultimately ending up at its island destination northwest of the country of Western Sahara. For eight days I heard nothing other than one communication with a brief coordinate update and a request to "push it out" to other people.

Just like any loving wife, I watched that dot on my computer screen and phone like it was my sole reason for living. I knew the wind speed, direction, wave heights, the names of every vessel around Jay, and just about everything else other than the meals he was eating. But dot watching becomes old after about day four, and I was getting colder just as the weather that Jay was encountering was becoming warmer.

That first leg wasn't a race to Gran Canaria—it was a sail under optimum circumstances on dates of the owner's choosing. Other than the risk of a particularly mean-spirited pod of Orca whales that were unnecessarily attacking the rudders of boats close to Portugal, loose fishing nets, and some freighters, it was a moderate risk operation. Even if Jay became very ill, they were surrounded by boats and very close to land at all times. He'd get medical care in a hurry.

Something told me as I watched the dot move that perhaps I needed to worry less about Jay being there, and more about me not being there.

Jay called when he arrived at the marina, full of excitement about the new friends he was making. We rarely travel apart, and I was anxious to join him before all of his new experiences, like Marco Polo's, became too much for me to digest.

I began to count the hours until Jennie and I would fly to meet him.

The Canary Islands are located off the coastline of West Africa, 62 miles from Morocco. Despite its proximity to Morocco, the archipelago remains a semi-autonomous region of Spain. There are eight islands, the two main ones being Tenerife, and Gran Canaria. The latter island was where the race would begin and where the rental apartment was located. It's the sub-tropical climate with masses of Canary Island date palms and beaches that lure millions of visitors a year, while for centuries past it was primarily known as a trading link between the continent of Africa and Europe, later including North and South America.

Gran Canaria wasn't what I expected; I had imagined that it would be like a cross between the Bahamas and the Virgin Islands. I can't speak for the rest of the island chain, but Gran Canaria is most like Hawaii in its volcanic topography, diverse population, beaches, and modern infrastructure.

The weather was always nice, the beach pleasant, and the breezes blowing. We didn't have air conditioning, but it was cool at night.

Jennie picked out the apartment we were to stay in on Gran Canaria the week before the race—a small apartment on the well-known Las Canteras Beach. It was totally unlike the nearby city of Maspalomas, with its beaches that attract masses of visitors in high-rise hotels, apartment complexes, and expensive gated subdivisions, capped off with endless tourist attractions, all stuffed together at the south end of the island.

Las Canteras was a locals' type of place. Retro apartments were remodeled into simple condos, and older hotels that have stood the test of time still look the same as they did decades before. There were no mini-golf courses or amusement parks; everything was authentic Gran Canaria. It turned out to be in the perfect location we had desired— nestled within an older part of the city, but only a short walk to the fancier malls, harbor, and the boat in the marina. Best of all, the golden sand beach was a surfer's paradise, giving us free sports entertainment from our balcony.

We swam each morning in the clear, clean waters off the beach, wandered to a bakery for local pastries, shopped in the afternoon, and spent the evening in Old Town. We visited the sand dunes and drove up the mountains. There was something for everyone on the island— so much so that Stephan, our German exchange student from a decade past, flew in to visit us for several days, a welcome respite from his work.

Having the apartment in town made it easier for me to shop for various items I was requested by the owner's wife to buy for the regatta, as if on a scavenger hunt, not a working mission. It was great to have Jennie wander the city with me while Jay attended to other matters. Plus, she was fun and up-lifting. I needed her laughter when I began to worry out loud.

It wasn't just the fear factor of the ocean that bothered me. After Gibraltar I had received many e-mails from the other two women about the meals on board and provisioning of the boat that were different from our summer discussions. While I was at home, they only made me feel off-kilter. However, shortly after my arrival in Gran Canaria, it sunk in that the provisioning decisions and shopping lists for the crossing were already chiseled in stone and my input was superfluous.

"So, basically it will be you two in the galley and three would be too many?" I finally asked the new crew member during a discussion over the never-ending topic of butter. I blithely threw in the question, expecting her to tell me that I was dead wrong—we would all work together.

"Well, yes," she said. "We think that."

I took a deep breath and said nothing. What could I do?

I shouldn't care that I didn't really have a role. Who cared who cooked or made provisioning decisions?

Ordinarily I didn't like to be role-less, though. I've never been role-less.

As Jennie read all the e-mails about provisioning being sent to me while the other women were stateside, she agreed to help me search for obscure items that they wanted so I wouldn't be stressed that I had failed them in some way. Instead of swimming she wandered for hours, guided by Google Maps, in order to find a store that sold us three jars of Ghee butter for $81.00. Once we finally secured the butter and could move on to other things, we cheered as if we had won a marathon.

All the while Jay downplayed my worry. "Just relax and let them do it all," he said, as he worked preparing fishing lines. "Really, just relax and enjoy yourself."

That was my plan.

Chapter Twenty-Four

J ay and I spent our free time wandering the marina just as we've wandered docks across the world—only this time we were trying to memorize our competitor's boat names. Supposedly there were three other Americans on a boat, but I never saw them until we reached Cape Verde. Around us were Germans, Norwegians, French, Brits, Swedes, and others from even further away.

At the time both the ARC and the ARC Plus boats were on the docks with their ARC flags and halyards flying colorful rows of signal flags. About a fourth of the boats were catamarans similar to our boat in size and manufacturer, almost all brand new or nearly new. The monohulls were on average much older except for one group that I couldn't gauge because they were in such pristine condition that they could have all been new. Those were the monohulls over fifty feet that were on a separate dock away from us. They were big sailboats with high-dollar price tags.

Crew members on those boats—the Oysters, Amels, Moodys, and Hanses—were making the same preparations that we were, eating at the same restaurants, and drinking at the same bars. They even wore the same Helly Hanson clothes. But they weren't like us. The owners were richer—much richer. Not all of them were necessarily wealthier than our owner, but they had definitely accumulated more wealth than Jay and me.

Many of the ARC Plus boats were bought for the sole purpose of this trip, and fully provisioned with supplies and crew. One owner strutted around so proudly that we called him the Baron. Others were completely self-absorbed, hardly interested in other crews or boats.

It didn't matter to me whether we spoke to these owners or not. The sailing yachts were all eye-candy to someone who didn't live a daily life around them, so I took endless pictures and sent them home.

Jennie and Stephan left several days before we were set to sail, much to my dismay. When we dropped them off at the airport it was as if two bright light bulbs went off, and suddenly I was acutely aware that I was facing a month and a half without seeing the children and grandchildren. But I quickly shook it off. I had made a promise, and I intended keep it. Plus, I had already bought the $500 life vest inscribed with my name in permanent marker.

Jay wouldn't go without me, and without him the owners would be in a fix, even if they didn't know it. I saw the type of people wandering the docks, wanting to jump on ARC boats as crew at the last minute. They looked like they could be trouble. Young healthy men and women willing and able to climb the mast and qualified to trim the sails and work the fore deck already had a life and were unlikely to spontaneously hop on a boat for six weeks.

Still, I worried. The newness of the boat could be more of an issue than I expected, beyond the fact that the kinks hadn't all been worked out—I found myself constantly worried about making that first scratch.

Perfection is a trap. There is an underlying level of stress that exists in every movement—a subliminal apprehension about when and how the yacht will undergo its first marks of age and thus its value drop. Days checked off the calendar quickly become the enemy. Sometimes a boat becomes too precious for the owner to share with family and friends.

I've been an owner and co-owner of boats my whole life, so I know that boats aren't the end-all and be-all of my life. I know that they get scratched, they become unloved, they betray you at the worst moments, and they don't define where you have made it in life.

Sometimes, just when you love them the most, they get blown away in a hurricane. But the good news is that I also discovered long ago that there is always a bargain for someone seeking a great used boat, one that was once the love of another owner's life.

The real concern should have been the sailing of a new boat. The multihull has a very large feel, especially when docking and reefing the mainsail. It's a lot for a novice sailor to absorb and feel at ease. That is why the Coast Guard requires years of experience from an applicant before he or she can even qualify to take the captain's test. Captains should not only be smart, but they should possess the right levels of confidence, disposition, and skills.

Owners don't have to be licensed United States Coast Guard captains, and most usually aren't. On the flip side, most captains aren't owners. With *Gypsy Lady*, however, Jay is both owner and a USCG captain.

A person in charge of a boat who is not a captain is called a skipper. Owners are usually skippers. There are a lot of differences in how the boat operates between an owner/skipper and a paid captain.

The most obvious of those differences is fun. Paid captains survive only when the guests and owner are having fun. The opposite is not true. Paid crew members aren't in it for the fun and they know it. I learned on the early Key West trip that perhaps unpaid crew members shouldn't expect to have fun either.

Benjamin Franklin often used a ship's captain as a metaphor for future leaders of the country, offering lots of advice on the subject. According to the January 15, 2014 article by John L. Smith, Franklin's "Top 15 Items to Take on a Cruise," the revolutionary hero who first mapped the Gulf Stream, said this about captains:

Regarding the ship's captain, Franklin told the reader that you cannot always 'make a choice in your captain.' But he added that if you could, it would make all the difference in making the closeness of a very long cruise miserable or 'so much the happier.'

Captains aren't the only important thing on a sailboat. Provisioning also matters. From the time early man first signaled to his mate that he might not be home for dinner and took off for the unknown in a dugout canoe with only a pouch of berries and nuts for sustenance, the idea of provisioning a boat has grown from small seeds into an art form. And I'm pretty sure that unless a charter company prepares identical boats for identical itineraries, no two boats provision alike.

It just so happened that while in Gran Canaria I went to the Christopher Columbus Museum and bought a small 6" x 9" book that explained and elaborated on the journal entries of his travels, all of which were connected to the Canary Islands. It is entitled, coincidentally enough, Christopher Columbus and the Canary Islands, and was written by Manuel Lobo Cabrera in 2019.

A professor at the local university, Mr. Cabrera searched log entries from Columbus's trips each time he followed the trade winds south to

Cape Verde and then, about "when the butter melted," took a hard right and rode the waves to the mythical island west of Cape Verde that he believed existed. Actually, after the first trip he knew about the "new world," but the logs continued for the next three trips.

The point of the museum story is that Columbus—who, incidentally, fell in love with a smart and beautiful woman on Gran Canaria—had detailed provisioning lists for his trips. Items brought for the trip across the Atlantic from Gran Canaria to Cape Verde and then to the New World included barrels of sardines, anchovies, wine, cake, wheat, flour, olive oil, vinegar, cheese, a "highly substantial" amount of sugar, and at least on the fourth voyage, bacon. I could live on only the wine, cakes, cheese, and bacon for the two-week crossing, and in reality, probably a whole year.

Columbus's water came, not from a water maker, but a particularly suitable brackish pool of water in Maspalomas, which still exists on the southern side of the island.

On the second voyage he added live animals including, young calves, sheep, goats, and hens. Out of boredom, I voted to also bring hens and a goat, but was outvoted by even my husband. That hurt. We had an empty stateroom perfect for live animals, and given the intensity of the provisioning, it seemed natural to hedge our bets and include animals that produced eggs and milk.

Several centuries after Columbus, Benjamin Franklin had many crossings under his belt when he compiled his suggested list of the top fifteen things a passenger should bring on a cruise. These included clean water, tea, coffee, chocolate, "good wine you like," raisins, almonds, sugar, lemons, Jamaican spirits, eggs, bread, and soup. Franklin wrote his list because, he opined, there is only a "small chance" that the captain will bring "good" food. I wondered where he stored it all.

Many of the items from Columbus and Franklin remain on provisions lists today.

Our provisioning began after Jennie left. The owner's wife and I used a detailed list emailed to her from the third couple. They would not arrive until a few days before we left Gran Canaria. Over the following week I spent hours with the owner's wife pushing full grocery carts while she picked out enough non-refrigerated staples to fill seventeen large boxes, including thirty pounds of flour, all of which were lovingly packed by a team of cashiers and thereafter delivered by the store. It was a decadent service provided for the yachting industry. In the following days we bought that same amount again, this time divided into smaller shopping excursions. Those trips included more refrigerated goods, meat, fruit, and vegetables.

Those who are provisioning a boat and don't do it on a regular basis, have a lot of self-imposed stress on their shoulders. They have visions of a food shortage disaster that will occur in the middle of the sea, dazed hungry men stumbling around on deck with ribs showing and blotches of blue on their lips like zombies. The reality was that dying of starvation on a forty-six-foot sailboat was not one of the top twenty risks of an ocean crossing in the 2020s. Over-shopping was usually more of a problem.

At some point I couldn't reconcile in my mind the sheer volume of food that we had bought, especially staples. From what I knew of their lives, the two women planning the provisioning had been spared the experience of spending every other Saturday morning shopping for two weeks-worth of food for six people, while I had done this for decades on end. That experience gave me a frame of reference as to what might be needed. I was confident that we'd never eat all the food we bought for the crossing, especially since we had also stocked loads of peanut butter from home, the preferred food of choice for most of us.

I didn't insist they leave anything behind. I was superstitious enough to know that the sea gods would punish me by ensuring that the item left behind was the one thing we ultimately needed to save our lives.

Because the carts were overflowing with provisions from the other women's lists, I wasn't allowed to buy anything extra. For good or bad, I had to forget adding things like rich and caloric European chocolate cookies to the basket. Instead, we bought lots of unseasoned dry bread snacks and dry wheat fiber cookies that had less packaging. We bought only a handful of soft drinks and juices, and we planned to only drink water from the water-maker.

There was definitely no wine aboard, something that I thought was a good idea. If the full-length mirror on our boat caused me to lose weight, the crossing had the potential to be ten times more effective.

The food purchased for the crossing was, to the extent possible, removed from its original unnecessary packaging and re-packed into reusable plastic bags before we left Gran Canaria. I brought a new vacuum sealer from the states for the bags that held meats and cheeses.

We removed the store packaging to ease the burden on small islands that we would visit with our waste, and to avoid transporting bugs aboard from the cardboard boxes. It certainly wasn't because of a lack of storage space.

New catamarans have so much storage that it's mind-boggling. When we were cruising for a week and eating out most meals there wasn't much food on the boat, and it was all stored in a few cabinets in the galley area. Most cabinets were empty.

On our crossing, however, food was stored everywhere—in the spaces under the salon seats, in the outside cabinets, over the sink and under the stovetop, in spaces under the floorboards, in the dry bilge spaces and the empty ice chest, and even in large crates in the empty stateroom on the owner's side, which I was reluctant to enter. We had a rudimentary map to identify where everything might be, but sometimes food was moved. If an item was moved and I didn't know it, I assumed that the food was gone—eaten, thrown away, etc. Of course, I was often wrong, finding that it had magically reappeared when I no longer wanted it.

Chapter Twenty-Five

C ooking wasn't the only social activity on most boats, but other than sailing it turned out to be the main one on ours. That was because the new crew member was researching and keeping a journal of the meals she prepared on board, using her American recipes—something I only learned after we left Gran Canaria.

As with any serious plan around a single topic, the idea of food in general became all-consuming for the other two women on board. They quietly pored over an iPad in the mornings and before dinner each night, and later spent hours on the meal preparations. Then the other husband walked around the table before dinner taking pictures of each night's meal.

Before leaving the states, and without understanding the limited access I would have to the galley or input on meals, I packed American provisions not available in Europe. I pre-measured ingredients for items to be cooked, like a caramel cake and pecan pie, pancakes, and cookies, and added Key West seasoning, fine vanilla extract, and quality spices, stuffing each of them into our duffel bags. Those sweet and caloric ingredients show where my mind was.

On the other hand, when the new crew member opened her luggage after she returned to the Canary Islands, she pulled out gallon-sized Ziploc bags with evaporated milk and ingredients for home-made yogurt.

I knew then that we were from different planets.

Cooking or not, I was convinced that no matter what happened on the crossing, I'd be okay because I'd have the ability to get emails and occasional pictures of the new babies over the boat's satellite phone at least once a day. Even without pictures, there would be constant daily reminders that I am loved and that I have a life at home to return to. However, after the Gibraltar incident and prior to leaving Gran Canaria, I worried that the boat's phone might have too many limitations, and I wanted my own satellite phone on board for that purpose. I was promised that I wouldn't need one. There would be plenty of communication, I was told.

I also knew from the start that boredom was one of the biggest complaints about the crossing, so I bought watercolors and paper, journals, playing cards, several books, and downloaded more books and movies (the movies were way harder than I thought). I recalled that there were board games on the boat like Yahtzee. On past sailing trips we had played riddle and word games and enjoyed lively discussions about current events and the books we were reading. At a minimum, if anything interesting happened I could write about it, as I had new empty journals.

I didn't bring music or headphones, since the boat had a great sound system and I had loved the play list we used all summer. There were too many other things to do for me to waste time making a new playlist or bring our own speakers.

It would all be fine. What I needed was for the race to get started.

The fireworks announcing our impending departure ended at ten the following evening, but unlike past regattas I've attended where crews were already wasted and parties just beginning, the enormous marina was eerily quiet. Most of the last-minute details were completed for our boat. Perhaps other tasks were destined to be left undone, only to weigh on the minds of captains and crew. Maybe the quiet was due to concern over the anticipated poor weather for the start. Whatever it was, the usual sense of revelry wasn't there—perhaps the winds had consumed it.

Winds were already blowing at the predicted 26 knots and gusting over 35 in the early morning. Flags and pennants were plastered across the sky. Everyone knew that the exit of 76 large sailboats from the marina in the man-made harbor would be crowded, notwithstanding a slightly staggered start. Waves were predicted to be over ten feet once outside the jetties, even if the wind moderated to a perfect 20 knots. I voted to wait a day for better weather, but it wasn't a democracy and no one even took notice of my vote. The regatta would start on the day it was planned, with parties in Cape Verde set in stone—weather be damned and full speed ahead.

Of course, I should have known about the weather earlier. Apparently, in another failure to watch the news, I missed the memo that Wanda, a well-formed tropical storm, was churning away hundreds of miles northwest of us. The problem was that her waves did not diminish much over time and distance. They continued across the Atlantic as giant swells from their origin in the storm until they hit land. While the thought of them rendered me quiet, I knew the surfers on the beach were thrilled, dreaming about riding the high, curling waves—or dreading, as sometimes happens, slamming their faces into the sandy bottom, sending their fiberglass boards home in pieces.

A ten-foot swell would equal or exceed my past experience in the Gulf of Mexico. All the Dramamine in the world couldn't quell the uneasiness I was feeling over the enormous waves I envisioned, monstrosities worthy of a Cecil B. DeMille movie, engulfing everything in their path.

Once again, I wondered, "why, oh why am I doing this?" Would it really be the trip of a lifetime, a notch on my belt? Given the lack of genuine interest from others about the travels I had made by plane to places like Petra, Malawi, and Hong Kong, I wasn't sure that this sail would be a life-changer in that sense.

As I wrote a final note home an hour before the race, using the Internet at the Sailor's Bay Bar at the end of the dock, I could already hear the wind howling. How could it do this to me? For a month the forecast had been a perfect 68 low and 76 high with consistent, moderate trade winds and gentle swells. Now this. All the while, my friends from home were sending me notes of encouragement such as "fair winds" and "hope the wind is behind you" which only made it worse. I knew that you never taunt the wind gods.

I was right. An hour later the swells outside the harbor were up to twelve feet. I once again asked (rhetorically), "why, if this is supposed to be fun, can't we leave tomorrow?" At the same time, I knew that the stripped-out racing boats were barely able to wait for the start.

There's a good reason that some sailboats cross at the same time as the ARC boats but aren't registered in the ARC, and therefore don't have to pay fees or buy all the specific safety gear that the ARC requires. These boats are referred to as "NARCs," since they are NOT participating in the ARC crossing. They are looked down upon by the ARC, but there is a lot to be said for the flexibility to leave on one's own terms in the optimal weather window, yet have company across the sea.

When we sail at home, even in a regatta, weather ultimately controls what we do. If there is a red blob on the weather map predicting a major front or storm in the next few days, we change our plans. An unexpected storm can always happen, and we will always be prepared for one. We don't go searching for trouble—it's not fair to those who may have to rescue us.

But this was a different situation, so go we did, exiting the harbor at 1:45 p.m. on a blustery Sunday afternoon, sailing along in a parade through massive jetties of concrete and rock. The jetties had spectators perched on top, waving flags, wishing their loved ones good-bye, or just sight-seeing and dreaming of the day that they too would take a trip to the other side of the enormous pond on which they lived.

I often felt like the latter group, remembering my feelings of pent-up frustration and desire when I gazed out my living room window due south across the Gulf towards Cuba, wondering when, if ever, I could sail there. It was a place connected to me by an unimpeded rhumb line, often driven by a north wind, interrupted only by politics.

The enthusiasm of the crowds humbled me to the core and my eyes teared up. Never a celebrity, sports star, or beauty queen, I understood for a moment how such figures must feel when they receive the sincere adulation of strangers.

Chapter Twenty-Six

*O*ur start was bumpy, but not as bumpy as the boats that hoisted their spinnakers and parasails only to have them immediately overpowered by the wind. Some were forced to reduce sail, others incurred damage, and the rest moved way off course. The decision to go only with the small self-tacking jib was not a racer's call. But like the horse, Secretariat, despite our slow start we were able to make a better course through the wind acceleration zone near the island. It was a risky move, but one that paid off. Once we rounded the island, Jay set our sails perfectly and we were in the chase for the lead.

The participants at the ARC seminars discouraged the multihullers from ever using the very large mainsail. They said it would serve little purpose down wind and it could be dangerous to deal with in rough conditions, as the boom was set high off the water and above the hard top on the big catamarans. We certainly found it difficult to reef. Therefore, all our drive would come from the Code Zero and self-tacking jib, along with ample freeboard to catch the trade wind off our stern the entire trip.

For the first two days we surfed the waves that rose and fell at our stern, at times propelling us so far down the wave's crest that we were invisible in the swells. We also raced ahead of seasickness, that uncomfortable nauseous condition occasionally nipping at our heels, ready to attack with the slightest provocation—reading, looking backwards, going below deck, eating…almost any act of daily living seemed a co-conspirator in an effort to make some members of the crew "green around the gills."

Jay and I wore Relief Bands for seasickness on the first days, which made us very comfortable under the worsening conditions. For reasons I couldn't fathom, the others on board saw the bands that, admittedly, looked like cheap fake-looking watches, judged them as a sign of weakness, and preferred to be sick.

The winds gusted at thirty knots while we were under the influence of the Canary Islands—winds strong enough and sustained enough to make me wonder if it was humanly possible to take a month at sea if the conditions did not improve. It was only when we exited the wind acceleration zones off the Islands that conditions moderated, and we were able to put up both the jib and the Code Zero on opposite sides. As it turned out, Wanda, our turn-around storm, helped to generate more favorable wind and wave direction.

Both forward sails furled, although the Code Zero required a man on the foredeck to deploy it or bring it in. The Code Zero is used only in light wind, less than twenty knots, so it wasn't ordinarily a dangerous operation to take it in or let it out. It was the sail of first choice due to its size and high clew.

We were able to sail wing-on-wing, also called the angel wing formation, with our jib and Code Zero on different sides, knowing exactly how the configuration would perform. The other sailboats in our vicinity were operating under a conventional set up of main and forward sail on the same side.

It was a while before the sailboat closest to us realized why we were leading them and changed sail configuration to match ours, but by then we had pulled away from the pack and catapulted to 14th place, overall. Jay was already obsessed with trimming the sails to their optimum advantage.

The reality is that Jay loves to race. Over time we have discovered that whenever two sailboats are within sight of each other they instinctively race, match wits, trim sails, and compare skills. They are incapable of any other behavior. The ARC is called a crossing, but no matter how much they profess that it is a regatta, make no mistake—if you have any chance to place then it is a race. It was only referred to as a rally when a boat was not doing well.

Given the fact that we weren't on an Oyster—didn't have the Rolex sponsorship and were without a paid professional crew—it hadn't dawned on me that we would actually have an opportunity to place.

By the end of day two the wind began to die, but we were moving well, the right amount of wind and following seas. We moved up to 11th position.

Day three the winds began to die. 5.0…4.8…5.1. By day four there was no wind at all.

In the ARC a skipper can use the boat's engine for one-third of the race, or some other vague calculation that I never quite understood. The penalties applied for engine use were equally nebulous. Since the goal of ARC was to get everyone to Cape Verde in time for the cocktail hour and parties, it was apparent that speed trumped method.

As Americans we aren't generally accustomed to the civilized British rule that dictates that a skipper can fire up the engines in a race, so it was difficult to know the exact timing for it. In our case the owner decided it would be when the boat speed was below 3.8 knots. The actions of other boats would be considered as well—good old peer pressure. If no one else was using the engine, then we would wait as long as possible.

This was why I was always watching the AIS tracking site on our computer, noting the exact moments that our closest competitor turned on their engine. Little blue dots that extended from the boat icon like Pinocchio's nose signified a huge increase in speed. We carefully calculated the time, speed, and distance and decided it was too early to follow their lead and turn on the engine, given the maximum time we could motor.

Two hours later, the speed wouldn't top more than 4.8 knots. We cranked up the engines and banked on our hopes for stronger winds on day five. I carefully took pictures of the engine gauges and times for the ARC officials to document our usage.

For the rest of the trip, we allotted our time between sailing when possible and using the engine when needed, never exceeding the one-third engine rule. The activity and excitement of competition filled Jay's and my days and minds. Boredom wasn't an issue. Any troubling patterns that might have emerged during daily life aboard were obscured by the fun and camaraderie of a close race.

There was a great sense of satisfaction when we entered the Cape Verde harbor and immediately filled up our fuel tanks, giving the ARC a definitive number of engine hours used. We were escorted from fuel docks to the first row of boats, a sign to anyone that our crew had performed well. In fact, no boat with a higher rating finished ahead of us, and the only other contenders had used their engines much more than we did.

It was as exciting as if we had won the Derby. Not only that, but we held that dock position with the leaders for a whole week, a sign of cool boaters.

The only downside was that we didn't understand, that the engine use percentage rule was not really enforceable. In fact, it appeared that cheating was rampant. We utterly failed in that endeavor. A boat with cute little children on board was with us the whole time and crossed the finish line not long after we did. I knew to the minute the engine hours they used, but its captain claimed only a small fraction of those he actually used. The toddlers hadn't cheated, just the skipper, but it still took a while for me to get over it and be able to tease and joke with them once more.

This was discouraging, but hope sprung eternal that we would win the second leg.

Chapter Twenty-Seven

We sailed into the harbor between two of the nine inhabited islands that comprise the Cape Verde archipelago, small volcanic islands sprinkled together due south of the Canary Islands and west of Western Sahara. It's hard to believe that they were uninhabited until the Portuguese took possession of them in 1462 and controlled them until 1975. Because the islands had no steady supply of water and were mostly barren, they weren't considered fit for human life before that.

The slave trade changed things. Ships began to use the stop-over in order to sell or abandon slaves that were too ill or deemed unfit for the longer trip to the west. It was cruelty that started the island's population growth.

The Portuguese did little to help the infrastructure, as the safe harbor and military vantage points were all they cared about. At one point they hired the locals to build brick roads by hand, which are still the main arteries on the islands, especially on the island of São Vincente. The reason for the roads? Military use, a reason to employ the locals who were starving, or so that early British visitors had somewhere to ride their horses—we were told all three versions by different guides on one of the trips arranged by the ARC committee.

The city where the marina was situated, Mindelo, is as African as Gran Canaria is Spanish. Other than a few westernized places near the marina, it was much like the capital of Malawi, Africa, but it was Portuguese, not British. Large, old colorful buildings in the Portuguese colonial style anchor the city center, almost all in a state of benign neglect. They are interspersed with hundreds of small shops, cafés, businesses, and markets, all rising gently up the mountain above the harbor. The entrepreneurial spirit is alive and well in Cape Verde.

Some days I saw as many as a hundred women perched atop stools on sidewalks along the roads that led to the "African Market," selling an array of enticing vegetables and just as many fish (not on ice). The actual outdoor square known as the African Market is a sprawling maze of permanent vendors selling hand-made jewelry and art, colorful clothes, and occasionally ordinary items a person might need.

Within the African Market there were also small open-air stands with men sitting out front sewing clothes on vintage Singer sewing machines that were older than I was. It stopped me in my tracks. I'd seen men in the same situation in Africa, but never seen sewing machines like those they used in Mindelo. They were from the Art Deco period, with lots of shiny chrome in elaborate designs, colorful enamel, and heavy steel bones, all in pristine condition—antique Cadillacs married to a simple sewing machine.

The brightly enameled machines reminded me of the very early boat motors with brightly painted engine covers, now highly collectable and seen as works of art. As someone whose grandmother was a seamstress and taught me to sew at an early age, I wanted to watch the entire process. The best way to achieve that was to have a skirt made, which I did—one of bright yellow eyelet.

I couldn't help but worry about the future of Cape Verde without a large influx of money to overcome the lack of natural resources, barriers to high school education, and other infrastructure needs. They were still dealing with past centuries of hard times, famines, and the still serious issue of potable water. On the upside, there are pockets where the middle class and tourism are beginning to take root, and they are growing fast. Tourists, especially groups like the ARC participants, help the economy in a multitude of ways, in the restaurants, food stores, marine shops, fuel docks, taxis, and tours.

The sailors didn't only spend their money in Mindelo, however.

Because we arrived early on the first leg of the regatta, we were able to join an ARC tour to another island, Santa Antao, to visit a factory where they produce grog (a local rum made of sugar cane) and then to tour its renowned beaches. The beaches were not just beautiful, but deadly, with perfect curling waves that hid a monster rip current.

Jay and I, along with the owners, took a ferry to the island and then hopped aboard a small modern minibus, which slowly climbed up a barren mountainside on a hand-laid brick road to the top. The destination was an old volcano crater. Once there we watched clouds pour over the rim like a waterfall generated by the power of the trade winds, and learned how the local residents used old and modern techniques to irrigate the experimental farms in the volcano's leftover bowl.

Minutes after we were refreshed with an ice-cold soft drink, we stood slack-jawed overlooking the greenest, lushest land I had ever seen. It appeared abruptly. Not far from the rim's edge on the highest point on the island, vegetation tumbled down to the ocean kilometers below. It wasn't just a small bit of land with trees and flowers; it was a panorama in every direction on the northern mountainside, cloaked in varying degrees of a rich deep green, punctuated occasionally by the lime color of new growth. It was shockingly dramatic after our time in the barren land on the other side of the mountain. One of the sailors on our bus described it as looking like Machu Picchu, where he had visited that summer. I believed him.

Silky, thin clouds lingered over the highest points, misting and feeding the land—clouds destined to be restrained within this beautiful rainy area, only rarely escaping to the mountain's other side. It seemed cruel that the waters avoided those who desperately needed them only a short distance away.

The sugar cane for the grog was grown in the wet region, along with bananas, avocado, and papaya. First a staple on Columbus's voyage, the sugar is now primarily used for the grog which is highly regulated and sold across the islands to locals and tourists. My only regret of the trip was that I took the dare to down my glass of grog in one gulp.

I was thrilled to be in Cape Verde—others not so much. Many owners were making major repairs to sails and riggings that were damaged in the crossing to Cape Verde, just like Columbus and many others had done before them. But it was the crewing issues that I was seeing and hearing about that interested me the most. It became clear that my joke about jumping ship in Cape Verde was a real thing.

The sweet mother who was crewing on a boat with her family—I saw her on the back of the boat scrubbing potatoes for the owners in what I can only describe as a humiliating and unnecessary operation. When she saw me dressed up, heading to the marina grill with Jay, this once gregarious woman smiled wanly and asked where I was going after Grenada. She volunteered that she wasn't going anywhere further. I didn't need to ask why—I knew the owner.

Then there was a female American sailor who lived in Europe and had signed on as crew on a boat of Germans, and was now bemoaning her situation. She said they were making her a slave on the boat, and she appeared absolutely miserable. I caught a glimpse of what she meant when they approached her as we were talking and told her "They had things for her to do." She shrugged slightly before they escorted her back to their boat.

Worst of all, I listened to the gazillionaire owner of an expensive new boat sitting at a table behind me in the marina café with his four male guests, plus a woman my age who may have been his wife. In an extraordinarily loud voice for the setting, he outlined his intention to get a new captain and let the current captain go on Tuesday "if he didn't change his attitude." I was shocked. After he trashed the captain over battery use, he said he also intended to talk to the captain's wife, who was the cook and everything else, and explain what he didn't like about the way she did things. He would tell her that "she needed to change."

The woman at the table tried to dissuade him from telling the captain's wife what he apparently had already told her on numerous occasions, but he was relentless. He said that he had spent "hours" preparing exactly what he would say to her.

Two days later the captain was gone—disposable. I am sure his wife went with him—at least I hope she did. I pitied their replacements on board.

I was beginning to see an ugly side of yachting. The ruptures, both personal and mechanical, on the other boats were spilling out onto the docks all around us. Not all wealthy owners were indifferent and not all crew members unhappy, and not all boats needed repairs, but suddenly there were enough issues to give me reason to pause.

Perception is often reality, and no more so than in sailing. Over the years I succumbed to the barroom theory that if you dress like a sailor, walk like a sailor, and quack out sailing stories, then you must be a sailor. I believed that if you own an Oyster 62 and are sailing across the Atlantic you must not only be rich (obviously), but a bottomless pit of sailing knowledge. I've even fallen for the stories of those leathery tan men who live on sailboats with names like *No Man's Land*, who talk like they're on the verge of circumnavigating the world, that is until you observe the potted plants on deck and years of marine growth clutching their hull, swishing to and fro as their boat gently rocks in the murky marina water.

Up until this trip I never owned a Helly Hansen jacket. In a little over six months Jay and I accumulated an entire line of over-priced marine wear, from jackets to bibs. Forget Columbia and West Marine—we'd gone global. Maybe I should have rethought some of those purchases before I put my name on them.

In a few short weeks with the ARC I learned a lot that challenged my assumptions. I'd never spent time around billionaires, but they were probably there with us in Cape Verde. They are different than the rest of us, or at least they want to be different. But they aren't happier on a quantitative level. They always need more—not an ordinary yacht, but a super mega-yacht, while most people achieve the same happiness with a boat of any kind.

Just like the employees who help them make all that money and keep it, they have crews as disposable as Pampers: maybe more so. They don't actually sail or clean the galley, and God forbid that they should evacuate the head.

As I mentioned earlier, not all yacht owners are aloof and imperious. Sailors and would-be sailors who worked hard and made money and bought their dream boat—they haven't forgotten life before wealth. They are kind to the people on their boats and in the marina. It is those who spend money to pretend to be sailors and make unreasonable demands of others that miss the mark.

At the end of the day money, or lack of money, in a marina is not always what gets a sailor's attention. It's the man with a beard and the best sailing tale, true or not, told in a deep, raspy voice, with a good stiff drink in hand like Ernest Hemingway, surrounded by a group of cruisers or racers hanging on every word while they sit at dives like the Sailor's Bay Bar or Last End Stop. Maybe, some in his audience think, one day I'll be rounding Cape Horn in an epic blow.

His listeners convince themselves that this bearded man, with no family and fewer responsibilities, must have a great life—-and maybe he does.

Chapter Twenty-Eight

We were in Cape Verde for a week, far too long unless we were having new sails flown in or parts delivered from the other side of the world. Columbus was usually trying to buy whole new ships at a similar point in his voyages. We used the time to swim half a day on a local beach. On a different day we rode up another mountain in a minivan, going around a hundred hairpin turns for no reason but to help the economy.

I spent many hours looking for specific food items that the cook wanted and more fresh sliced bread that everyone else wanted, which resulted in a children's game of sprinting from one shady sidewalk to another as I lugged heavy bags back to the boat in the hot sun. Jay spent his time quizzing locals on fishing and buying the lures they recommended.

As much as I loved Cape Verde, even the shopping, I was beyond ready to go by the time we left: ready to be on the sea, heading towards our final destination.

In the end, it was hard for me to reconcile the sweet islands and their kind residents with my lifelong association of Cape Verde as the incubator of all the hurricanes that threatened and damaged my home and community. According to meteorologists on the weather channel, Cape Verde generally spawned the systems that moved across the Atlantic and impacted the United States, Mexico, and other countries in the Caribbean.

There's nothing like a visit to the hurricane birthing place to get a better understanding of how they are created. Sailing the trade winds route only served to emphasize why the storms follow a fairly predictable path. I finally visualized the track of the Saharan sands, and how and when the wind carries them over the ocean. If the sands were thick and heavy, I saw how they slowed down the formation of the storms. On one windy day, we even had a light dusting of the fine sand on the boat. What once seemed to me mere guessing from afar was suddenly less voodoo and more science.

A ten-day out forecast didn't seem like such a stretch anymore.

I was pretty sure that in the future I would still groan when I heard the words Cape Verde—but now I'll add a slight smile at the end.

I missed its sweetness almost immediately after we threw aside our mooring lines and headed out to sea.

Toby Hodges writes in Yachting World, 8/17/2020, that a survey of the 276 boats from the previous year's Atlantic crossing revealed that "158 skippers said they experienced sail or rigging damage." and that "it's important to have a back-up system or means to repair a breakage."

Sails are like clothes for a sailboat; it's naked without them. It cannot move without a sail unless by engine, which then turns it into a dreaded power boat.

I wear clothes because it would be awful if I didn't. I have clothes for cold weather, hot weather, cocktail parties, beaches, fat days, and skinny days. The longer I live the more I have.

Similarly, Jay and have I sailed the Gulf long enough to know that we needed a plethora of sails, much more than I need additional clothes. There's really no such thing as too many. In addition to the ones on the boat, we have a sail bag in the trunk of my car, two in the hallway, one in the loft of the cabin, and another being repaired. We're also in the process of buying one, if not two more.

Sails are very expensive, and it takes time and money to build up a wardrobe, I mean inventory, of them. I doubt money is generally an issue for those in the ARC, but most of the boats on the crossing are new, and only experienced sailors can think through the maze of potential back-up sails that might be necessary.

That is why vendors at the ARC seminars recommended to the multihull fleet, mostly new boats, that owners put their trust into one light wind headsail—in our case the Code Zero. I went to enough of those seminars to know that the people selling those sails thought it was a perfectly grand idea.

The problem is that the crossing is in general downwind, with the wind blowing from only slightly off the stern. Given the direction we were headed, that meant it would jibe more easily. Even in light wind with perfect direction the sail begins to take stress from the continual sail set. The powerful popping of a jibe, especially if it occurred frequently, magnified the risk of too much stress.

That is one of the reasons that the Yachting World magazine article made it clear that tacking, or sailing on the angle, during a crossing is the way to go in order to avoid jibes. Plus, sailing on an angle is faster and more pleasant.

There is also the issue of de-masting on a catamaran if the wind in the forward sail is too strong. To protect themselves from the many lawyers who own those sails, the manufacturer of the boat installed a plate or sticker on the helm with strict reefing requirements that must be followed in order to keep the mast in place. Not to be out-done by the boat manufacturer, the creators of the expensive light wind sails— Code Zeros, Spinnakers, and Parasails—have their own set of maximum speeds which cannot be exceeded.

As a monohull sailor, I didn't fully appreciate at the beginning of the trip how serious the de-masting issue is for catamarans. I was only glad to know that thanks to some design improvements, pitch-poling is no longer as much of an issue as it was when Jay and I sailed the big trimaran to Key West when we were young.

The *Gypsy Lady*'s mast comes through the top of the trunk, then extends through the cabin and is ultimately stepped on the keel. When the wind comes at us in a gust it can blow the boat almost to the surface of the water, but the sails and hull are designed to allow the wind to spill out of the sail even before the toe-rail is submerged. Our boat has a full keel that draws only four feet and three inches, and also has a retractable bronze centerboard that we raise and lower with a "worm-gear" that is set in the stand of the salon table. Access to it is located under a small cover on the table top. We rarely have cause to use it, however, given how shallow the water is on the northern Gulf Coast.

At what always seems like the very last second before the boat tips over, gravity from the weight in the heavy keel pulls the boat back upright, much like a child's water-toy popping up from the bottom of a tub. It is scary or exhilarating based on your point of view—but it's also what monohull sailing is all about.

Catamarans operate differently. The masts are designed to sit on the top of the deck; they don't go through the deck of the cabin because there is no keel on a catamaran to support it. It has strong stays for support, but even so, I see it like a table umbrella. If all you do is place the umbrella in a shallow hole, the first gust of wind will blow it away. If, on the other hand, you have a pole that goes to the ground and is then weighted down at the bottom, the cloth may rip, but the pole will stay upright.

One way isn't necessarily better than the other; they both offer different risks and a different ride. The difference in the hull and mast configuration primarily means that a catamaran will not heel over. This is one reason that it was a little easier to live and cook on one. Catamarans can be constructed like condominiums with lots of staterooms and space. A guest can have glass wineglasses sitting on the countertop of a multihull—not so much on a monohull.

The most important difference is that mast or no mast, catamarans don't sink. That is one reason why multihulls that are intended for light cruising and ease of entertainment are increasingly the boat of choice in the Atlantic crossings.

Within twenty-four hours of leaving Cape Verde, four pivotal things occurred that would change our approximately two-week Atlantic passage and course, both figuratively and literally. One, we caught a giant blue marlin. Two, the Code Zero received a quarter-size perforation in it. Three, our boat distanced itself from almost every other boat participating in the ARC Plus crossing. Four, the wind began to die. Not in that order.

The winds were fluky, coming at us from different angles on the day that all the boats left the Cape Verde archipelago. It was frustrating because we would have fared so much better if we had just left a day or so earlier, or else several days later. Instead, as it was, the weather was changing, and we were heading straight into a very low-wind area of the ocean. Worse yet, the pocket of low wind was predicted to move with us as we meandered toward Grenada, keeping us trapped unproductively for days. As a result, we had the Code Zero up and kept the jib furled, trying to make some time while we had the opportunity.

We were also sailing the rhumb line which, in this circumstance, meant that the sail was having trouble keeping the wind.

Jay was at the helm, even though he wasn't on a scheduled watch. He noticed that the wind had shifted considerably and we could no longer carry the Code Zero on the heading the owner had set. The owner was below in the aft cockpit. As soon as the sail backwinded the first time Jay altered course and the sail popped back out with a loud thud when it refilled with wind. He asked me to summon the owner so that they could bring in and furl the Code Zero and then release it on the other side of the boat.

There was a delay in this process during which Jay continued to fall off the wind in order to keep the sail from backwinding again. This time the owner went to the foredeck instead of Jay. While considering the situation, he hesitated long enough that by the time he started pulling the Code Zero in, the sail backwinded a third time. This time it caught on one of the protruding metal bolts or pins at the clew of the furled jib, which perforated a small quarter-size hole in one of the Code Zero sail's membranes.

I could barely see the small hole, but at that moment, the owner and his wife, who undoubtedly remembered what they had paid for the new sail earlier in the year, instinctively reacted as if an act of sabotage had just occurred.

Chapter Twenty-Nine

*I*n the middle of the post Code Zero issue, the fishing rod that Jay had bought for the owner bent over and the Shimano reel sang like never before. It was like hitting the jackpot at a casino. The screaming line and the sudden emergence of a blue marlin tail-walking behind and next to the boat diverted everyone's attention. The fishing lure Jay had bought in Cape Verde attracted a beast, a real beauty with bright blue scales layered over a deep black background.

Once the great fish was securely on the line, the boat owner took the rod and reel from Jay and continued the fight to pull it in. The fight, man against fish, went on for hours, until well after dark.

By the time the fish was subdued I was dismayed to find that in that length of time we had distanced ourselves far away from almost all the other ARC boats. The rest of the fleet had sailed south to avoid the worst of the "light wind" pocket of air I referenced earlier. Suddenly, our safety net of near-by boats was gone. The safety in numbers was one of the main reasons that I had agreed to the crossing in the first place.

Oh my God, I wondered, what had I gotten myself into?

I watched the AIS monitoring system as the other boats—including everyone I trusted—headed south for better wind. The owner decided not to change course, however. He planned to follow the rhumb line as best he could manage all the way to Grenada.

Once the fish was conquered, the wind died, and the last ARC boat that I could monitor was too far south for me to detect on AIS, the owner was able to return his attention to the new Code Zero and its first injury. He had no back-up sail.

We had at least two weeks left to go.

There was no perfect Plan B for the tiny puncture in the Code Zero. The manufacturer that spent so much time delineating maximum wind speeds and other warnings failed to include a sail repair kit, and the owner didn't have one, other than a roll of clear white sail repair tape, similar to the stuff they use at the post office. It turned out to be sufficient to do the job, thankfully.

But it didn't stop the worrying. If the diameter of the hole grew and the sail failed, we would be limited to crossing the ocean with the small self-tacking jib. If we were forced to resort to that, it would be a very long trip indeed, as we did not have enough fuel to cross the ocean.

The wind completely died the next morning, and the owner wanted Jay to fish all day. Each day Jay rigged poles, set lines, and hooked amberjack and mahi, blue fin and yellow fin tuna. I had no idea there were so many fish in the middle of the ocean, or that they were such beautiful works of nature. If we were catching this many fish and also couldn't see another fishing boat for at least a hundred miles, then there could be some hope for the ocean's future, I thought.

The other two men would sometimes participate in gaffing the fish, but they always left Jay to fillet the catch and clean the blood off of the boat. He's an excellent fish cleaner but, again, no one really likes to clean fish.

I didn't blame anyone for not wanting to clean fish. Catching and cleaning fish necessarily involves some potent odors, and in Jay's case, those odors along with dried blood were embedded in his skin and clothes. Jay and I could only take showers when the generator was on and making water, and sometimes we were on watch when that occurred. After a couple of days, it was impossible for me to miss the smell of a fish market in our quarters.

We were several days into the trip before I had any real communication with the children, and then only for a short time. Patrick, a sailor, pilot, and schooled in meteorology, was our child best capable of understanding the systems on board the catamaran. I knew that just as he had watched and analyzed Jay's Gibraltar trip, he would watch and study every second of our trip, following the tiny dot that represented his parents in the midst of a big blue sea. Whatever he could do to keep us safe, he intended to do.

From day one, Patrick was able to discern that we were on the wrong track for his preference and our safety—we should be sailing south with the others. He didn't realize that the owner was following the ARC-provided weather and wave information which, although accurate when distributed, only extended for a three-day period. Given the length of the trip, Patrick was looking much further ahead.

As soon as we had some connection, he wrote us an e-mail and said that we needed to be searching for wind, planning our trip for the long game, and using the engine to get out of the windless zone if necessary. There was wind in the distance, and if we reached it then we could sail. I had watched or attended all the ARC classes on weather, and they never mentioned the long game. In fact, they were mostly selling the services of a personal meteorologist to guide the boat's trip day-by-day, someone the owner would pay to advise the skipper or captain. We had Patrick for free.

It wasn't a surprise that the owner relied on the three-day ARC weather reports, all of which began with a cheery British "Good day," even when it wasn't. They were the experts. He would stay the course.

When Patrick realized that we weren't going to go south or turn on our engine to power out of the low-wind zone drifting across the Atlantic with us, he began to send clever e-mails to amuse me once a day, knowing how I must feel. My favorite e-mails included the "sailing news" that one of the ARC boats left several days after the start and had already motored into the middle of the pack. The world news was about some "Omicron" COVID variant in Europe. I thought it was a joke.

But I never got baby pictures, and there was never enough writing space to say much. The boat's satellite phone was really for important or occasional use and never private. What would I say anyway?

That loss of communication subliminally tugged at my spirits. The days were becoming shorter and nights longer, and I wasn't sure what to do, much less what to write about. Blue skies and blue water?

It wasn't that the ARC didn't make it clear to us that boredom, which often fed crew discontent, was the one universal complaint. It was one of the many things the ARC did quite well. Yet as many times as they said it, I couldn't fathom the depth of the boredom and the consequences of it until I was experiencing it firsthand.

Benjamin Franklin spent great lengths to describe in his journals that feeling of aloneness while sailing. He noted that "one of the worst punishments is to be excluded from Society," and that those who profess to enjoy solitude for more than a short "refreshment" may not be so truthful.

There is a more recent and well-researched article about the universal issue of boredom during an offshore crossing entitled La Possibilita Di Un'Isola, or The Boredom in Offshore Sailing, by Fabio Brunazzi, June 24, 2018. In the article the author is brutally honest about the fact that all sailors encounter boredom, whether solo sailors or with others on board. What I learned from his research was that the monotony and claustrophobia from confinement in a fixed, small space looking at the same water and same sky each day, whether windy or in the doldrums, is a psychological challenge unlike any other. Not only is it the plot of many classic novels as well as great fodder for horror films, but it was also used on Alcatraz as a particularly cruel form of punishment for prisoners.

Some sailors use the crossing experience to exorcise a demon that they are mentally fighting —the more difficult their time, the better. But most sailors, and most of those on the ARC Plus with us, were really just looking for a pleasant trip. The challenges that I expected and prepared for were physical in nature, and I expected them to come from Mother Nature and the expanse of ocean. I ignored the warnings about the rest.

Chapter Thirty

*I*t just so happened that during the early part of the crossing Jay was reading Amor Towles 2016 book, The Gentleman from Moscow. In the book the main character finds himself confined to a hotel room for most of his adult life. Our stateroom became Jay's and my "hotel room." Once I left the comfort and security of our stateroom, I encountered the strange feeling that I was invading the owners' space.

My space was organized in my own way, and it was comforting. The other space was almost foreign, and I was constantly concerned about being intrusive.

Space didn't matter on the earlier "vacation" cruises that included dinner out almost every night, but when you can't escape for a moment, even for a swim, and when the outside spaces on the bow are too risky to occupy, the concept of space matters.

The aft cockpit with its large, fixed table and cushioned lounging was where I should have enjoyed the trip, but almost immediately once we left Cape Verde, I realized that two hundred square feet was not much at all. First of all, I had to be quiet during noon when the other man was using his sextant to experiment with sun sights, and then later in the midday, when he moved about the aft cockpit from the table to the top of the ice chests to make calculations.

The rest of the time the crew was told to keep their voices low near the open hatches around the aft cockpit just in case someone was napping. Although I could sleep through a freight train, others could not. I thought it was an odd request because a catamaran in a good wind with some decent speed groans like a wild animal, and hatches were everywhere, but I worked hard to be compliant.

One day the first week, when the wind wasn't blowing and the seas were calm, I laid out my watercolors on a cloth on the table in the aft cockpit. intending to paint each couple a simple painting from photographs I had taken in Venice. However, it was immediately clear from the owner's shocked reaction that the boat was still too new for any paints, water soluble or not. I didn't want the stress of an errant drop hitting the deck.

I'll never forget the silence aboard in the minutes after I carefully repacked my brushes, when the others resumed looking at their e-books and iPads. It was deafening.

Suddenly, I desperately wanted sounds other than those created by the boat's movement—but there were no other sounds. No matter how much I gently suggested it, the music on the boat never played, because the rest of the crew used earphones and their own play lists. It was a hard lesson learned. I highly recommend that if you are making a crossing that you shouldn't worry about life vests—get play lists instead.

It was important that I had something to occupy my mind other than endlessly reading, and I searched high and low for that something. I often offered to cook, but that was reserved for the other woman. Writing only works for me if I have something to write about, and most of my days were the same: wind and water and waves, occasionally punctuated by the appearance of dolphins or flying fish. It was great fodder for a poet, but not me.

Given the lack of options for entertainment, most of my time was spent on the back scupper watching the waves.

I've heard before that the size of your yard doesn't matter—what matters is the size of your view. Over the years I have believed it to be true, especially when we lived on the beach and our lot was small. But as I sat looking out to sea on the Atlantic, observing the vastness of the ocean and lack of any birds, people, or other boats, I occasionally had the odd feeling of claustrophobia. I wondered if it was how astronauts felt, or rather were trained not to feel. No matter how stunning the view, the lack of mobility or ready exit from the boat was as stifling as a broken elevator.

When that happened, I retreated to my safe space, the small stateroom, and shook off the feeling. Surely I was capable of mitigating these claustrophobic impulses by concentrating on the space between my ears—mind over matter. The issue was how to control those thoughts.

By the end of the first week, I felt like I was living full-time in a high school library with a no-nonsense librarian who allowed no music, no talking, no board games, no cards, no laughing, no passing notes, no holding hands, and definitely no painting. It was where bad students went for punishment.

That's when it occurred to me, the extrovert, that I had unknowingly been committed to the sea's version of long-term in-school suspension.

But it wasn't so with the introverts. They loved it, as so many sailors do.

About the same time as the flashback to junior high, I also recalled a video I had viewed about life aboard a multihull during a crossing. The video was suggested by the owner when we were going through the ARC training. At the time, I thought the behavior of that crew was not especially interesting or appealing, and put it out of my mind. They were mostly solemn and quiet while they read, gave small smiles at the camera and weak waves and did a lot of yoga stretches and pulls. Their quiet days were interrupted only by some fishing, a cook feeding them meals in dog bowls, and maybe a squall or two. The only real attention I paid was to the fishing and the fact that all the good snacks were gone in the first day or so.

In retrospect, I totally missed the message. It wasn't about fishing or snacks—it was about the allure of extreme quiet, lazing around reading books, napping, and doing chin-ups on the doorways. Maybe that was who we were supposed to be emulating.

The only thing I knew for sure was that by the time we left Cape Verde, we were the same but for the chin-ups. Perhaps this was how full-time living on a boat was supposed to be. It couldn't be fun every day. It was just life, but on a boat. Some people love to retreat to the country, walk in the woods, and never speak to another person all day. That's okay. Others, including me, might like a solitary day hike or overnight camping, but in general prefer to be surrounded by other people. For many extroverts, sailing is an activity to be enjoyed with others.

Neither way is better than the other, just different. Only, on our boat this difference was monumental.

Chapter Thirty-One

*I*t turned out that I did have one non-sailing role: washing dishes. Over the years when sailing with the owners I often offered to wash dishes, even when I cooked or helped with a meal, and especially when there were other guests on board. I did the same over the summer trip with the new crew members.

That was why it took a few days before I internalized that they expected me to wash everyone's lunch and dinner dishes every day. Before I could complain and change things, they were accustomed to eating and leaving me to clean. Like with the play lists, communicating when I would or wouldn't wash dishes was something I should have handled before the trip. I missed my window of opportunity to complain.

The biggest concern in a tiny galley, and they are all tiny by definition, is not the washing itself, but that there is little space to wash and clean, especially when items are stored on the counters. There is one moderately sized sink and no dishwasher. Because cooks often use every pot and pan and all of the serving dishes, plus plates, silverware, etc., for the meals, washing dishes in the galley loses any glamour that the dishwasher tries to give it.

My son, Harrison, told me that when he was with Teach for America, he and his three roommates each had one night a week to cook a meal. The arrangement included a caveat: whoever cooked the meal cleaned the kitchen. The cook could use every pot and pan in the house, but he or she would be the one to clean them and not leave them to someone else. If I could do it over again, I'd highly recommend that plan in writing right up front.

The ARC knew it was hard to keep crews happy and repeatedly recommended that they eat dinner together every night. The problem was that sometimes people just don't want to eat, including me. The food could be good or not—it didn't matter. When eating is your only activity, and you have little control over what it is or when it is served, food becomes less interesting at a minimum.

Mostly, I didn't do anything to make me hungry. Sailors are in general very fit, but it was impossible for me to get the same amount of aerobic exercise on the multihull as I did at home. Yoga wasn't enjoyable in cramped spaces and rolling waves. I wasn't swimming a mile or working on outdoor projects. Out of desperation, one day, I looked for a place to try chin-ups, but there was nowhere to do them.

Although I didn't plan to lose weight, I did. But I also could see how easily sailors could gain weight on a multihull, especially if they bring their favorite foods and drink for the voyage.

For the most part I sat on the stern by myself and contemplated how things had changed with the crossing. It was comforting to know that the towering waves were not my enemy, but rather the opposite of frightening, moving me to where I wanted to go. They slowly emerged from behind the transom and rose as they approached until they towered behind the stern of the boat, as high as the top of the davit, finally collapsing just short of the boat, leaving only a trail of white foam licking at the scuppers. The wind at our back propelled us forward just like it was meant to do—an exhilarating downhill sleigh ride off the coast of Africa. It was mesmerizing and calming to watch the predictability of the seas as they rose up and down, up and down, as the push of every large wave made the remaining trip shorter.

The big question always in my mind as I sat on the scupper and thought about the crossing was whether I would have signed on for an almost two-month-long isolating trip—much of it as a tiny speck on a huge and dangerous ocean—and missed our Bahamas cruise on *Gypsy Lady* and two of my granddaughters' early months of life, knowing that I would be washing dishes and whispering?

The crossing was such a startling departure from our past sailing experience that Jay felt the need to work with me on ways I could handle the quiet and boredom. He knew it was extremely hard. I might enjoy time alone, but I'm not known to voluntarily go on two-hour silent retreats, much less be quiet for over two weeks at a time.

Not being able to participate in the galley, and not even being allowed to turn on the oven or freely open refrigerators turned out to be harder on me than expected, as I love to cook. Like the play lists and the washing dishes, I immediately recognized the fact I should have been more assertive about the meals before departing, instead of optimistically thinking that it'd all work out. It was too late after we left the Canary Islands.

Jay told me that I shouldn't try anymore to change anything—just go with it and not rock the boat. I did the best I could to do as he suggested, however, that gentle comment revived in my empty head the lyrics "don't rock the boat baby." It began to play at the least provocation, echoing from ear-to-ear in the silence of the boat, eliminating any chance another song might reappear. Over and over again the words played, but only the first two lines. Unfortunately, or maybe fortunately, I didn't even know the rest of the song.

Chapter Thirty-Two

*T*he problem with going nowhere fast and counting all the boats in front of you, nursing a sick sail, and the twenty-four-hour quiet, was that small things become big things, especially when a raw nerve was hit. It was my nerve that got nicked early one morning.

I entered the aft cockpit and couldn't miss the other male crew member standing with his hands across his chest, leaning in his chino shorts against an outside cabinet, his glee only minimally concealed by the exaggerated frown on his forehead. I knew something was up. His blue eyes pierced my green ones from above his lowered reading glasses—those glasses not to be confused with the Ray Ban sunglasses perched on his head. My entry had interrupted the quiet of the early morning when everyone was leisurely enjoying their coffee.

Once I was too far into the area to retreat, his voice filled the void of silence like that of an unhappy principal at the microphone in the school auditorium. His exact words were:

"Did you use toilet tissue this morning?"

Half-way across the Atlantic Ocean while slogging along at the modest speed of 3.8, the inevitable had happened. A toilet, in this case, the one off my stateroom, had suddenly stopped working.

How many times had I seen this play out before? A head is clogged, and some poor girl is hauled out in front of the crew like a petty criminal or a Salem witch and humiliated so much that she hides in her cabin in shame, seasick and miserable, never to be heard from again.

Why is the woman always publicly shamed? There is never a discrete, quiet taking her off to the side to discuss the issue, protecting her dignity. No, it's always a spectacle, the woman's name and story repeated for decades by captains whenever the topic of a head arises. Men will say they don't need toilet paper, much less toilets, and they certainly are never surprised by an unexpected time of the month.

Over the past forty years I had witnessed the increased scolding and mocking of women, most of whom had little or no boating experience, after they used a boat's head and it later malfunctioned. I increasingly felt small when I was unable to adequately defend my fellow sex when surrounded by a group of laughing boaters seeking a funny story at someone else's expense. This time I was going to take up for women of the world—there would be no degrading. I stood my ground and looked at him straight in the eye.

"Yes, I have indeed used a square or two of one-ply marine grade toilet paper." Gauntlet down. After forty years of sailing, I wasn't so stupid as to stuff the head with enough toilet paper to clog it.

"Well," he huffed loudly as if dismayed at my answer, but in reality unable to hide his joy at the ease in which he obtained my confession, "My wife and I save all of our used toilet paper and then throw small brown paper bags of it over the side of the boat."

I had never witnessed them actually doing that, but it made sense. Why not furtively run around the boat discharging bags of used toilet paper at the boats behind us like tiny torpedoes, rather than allow small bits of expensive, marine-grade toilet paper to pass through the new pearly-white pipes that lead to the holding tank made for that specific purpose? Why should the owner and guests expect that in 2021, the head, macerator, and expensive marine toilet paper are fit for their only purpose in life? There is an environmental reason to always use marina toilets when on shore, but shouldn't a head be warranted to work offshore for all guests, men and women?

I stood quietly and ruminated about the unfairness of it all.

"Now, I hate to get on my soap box about this," he said solemnly, all eyes but mine on him as I looked for a soap box to hand him, "but we are a long way from shore, and we can't just get these parts when we break things."

He didn't know that Jay was the one who had carried replacement parts for the head from the US in our luggage, along with a suitcase of other mechanical items—just in case. Plus, we had four heads on board the boat.

"No problem," I said casually, not rising to his bait. If I was a smoker, I would have taken a drag. "I'll use a bucket. I'm a boater and adaptable."

No one said anything for a moment, including the boat owner. That wasn't reassuring. Despite the fact that the owner told me in the past that, on this very same topic, he didn't want us to be "bohemian"—it was a new yacht after all—he nodded intently in agreement with my accuser and then said that he, too, along with his wife, who nodded in agreement, were also throwing toilet paper overboard. I was shocked that after several weeks, neither Jay nor I had witnessed the flow of toilet paper in brown bags off the stern of our boat like a mini Mardi Gras parade. We would have happily added another row ourselves.

With that news my accuser went on a soliloquy of the horrors that I had wrought.

I stood there alone on the chopping block, stuck in suspended disbelief as he waxed eloquent about dirty toilet paper for at least ten minutes. As much pent-up frustration as I had at that point, I still had enough smarts to know that half-way across the ocean is no place to hook it up with anyone, so I swallowed the retorts bubbling up inside me like magma in a soon-to-erupt volcano.

It made sense that the owner was concerned. No one wanted to fix a head, but I was equally sure they weren't enamored with the idea of me sitting on a bucket and then slopping it across the decks at breakfast time, probably dribbling a bit when I threw it overboard.

I actually began to perversely look forward to the spectacle—it would send out an entirely new statement about yachting.

It was clear to all that someone had to inspect the toilet, but the three men suddenly professed that they knew nothing about toilet plumbing. Even better, the little each one knew was probably less than the man on either side.

They reluctantly decided to jointly tackle the issue together. They formed a line, a sad little marching band with a toolbox as a tuba and the accuser as drum major, and descended the steps to the head that I used—which, for the record, was quite clean. I felt sorry for Jay. He didn't dare offer to try and fix it himself at that point.

Anyway, the toilet was so clean that in less than a minute the owner had turned the rotator in the toilet base with a screwdriver, and, voila, it worked. I believe that a tiny piece of round plastic had clogged it up—

most likely the very same plastic that came from the tips of the bristles of the toilet bowl brush.

"For future reference," I was told by the owner that I should know that "anything—even a small undigested olive pit or small watermelon seed—can stop the plumbing from working." Interesting, if not timely, information.

The cleaning discovery, of course, led to another teaching moment.

"In the future make sure you just use a tiny piece of toilet paper to clean the toilet and wipe the bowl," Jay told me, using exaggerated hand gestures in circular motions while pointing to the bowl. Thereafter he said I should dispose of the tissue into the tiny covered bin that I had thoughtfully bought before the trip began.

Finally, he reminded me to wash my hands.

I laughed for the first time in days—quietly, of course.

Chapter Thirty-Three

*A*ll three couples aboard had maintained long-term marriages. I had no idea how the other two navigated their lives together at home, or where their fault lines lay. It was only important to me that Jay and I kept our act together while on the crossing.

When I felt low, I clung to the fact that Jay and I were always teammates. Love, empathy, and kindness didn't exit our lives when the sails went up or the seas were rough.

Not all the couples we had met in our years of sailing operated the same way. Over the years I've found that couples respond to the stress of sailing together by either bonding together or spectacularly blowing apart.

We were a young married couple when we saw firsthand that sailing can aggravate some couples' tiny fissures until they erupt over something that on the surface seemed innocuous. It was at the end of a perfectly wonderful seven-day sail in paradise on a 57-foot Irwin sailboat when the longest-married and seemingly most stable couple aboard engaged in a loud and ugly fight in the middle of the main shopping street in St. Thomas. While the rest of us were shopping for earrings, they were permanently undoing what a priest did many years before—and they were doing it in the middle of a road full of shocked tourists. They pledged to divorce and never speak again. We never saw it coming.

They never returned to the boat in St. Thomas, and Jay and I moved into their stateroom. We never learned why they had divorced. It made no sense; we were in one of the prettiest places in the world, on a great boat with plenty of room and a super captain. Was it something that happened on the trip or was the trip intended to save the marriage and the attempt failed? All I know is that we were so impacted that we pledged to avoid letting any simmering anger fester that might ruin a good shopping trip.

Because of that experience I still cringe when I hear couples act unkindly to each other on boats, as is common in the transient slips beside us in the harbor at home. Usually, they yell about some mistake one of them made that wasn't really worth arguing about at all. But too much drinking, too much risk taking, and too much or not enough money can expose and tear open a hairline fracture when on a boat. The cause can be one big thing or a million small things, but I saw too often where too much togetherness and blame assessment explodes like a gas engine that wasn't properly vented after fueling.

It's far easier to take a breath and be rational about daily dings and scrapes, than it is to take back ugly words said in the heat of the moment. Most sane people don't loudly curse their spouse at the mall because they scratched the door of a new car, so why on earth would the same person act that way on a boat in front of the dockmaster and other boaters?

Which brings me to alcohol: besides impairing senses on a passage where anything can go wrong on a moment's notice and you always need your wits about you, when it comes to tenuous relationships, drinking is like throwing lighter fluid on a simmering fire.

I think it might be best to save the drinking for times you can walk away. Or at least swim away.

Under the best of circumstances, it's hard to stay upbeat all the time. One afternoon Jay and I were lying on our berth in the heat of the midday without a hint of breeze our way, looking up to the open hatch above us as the small white clouds wafted by. We both felt lost and wished we were home. Something about that particularly long, hot afternoon when we were still moving slowly and felt destined to drift across the sea for eternity, caused us to begin our first serious talk since the Code Zero incident.

For hours we lay there and talked softly in the stifling space (the generator wasn't to be used other than to occasionally charge the house batteries), eventually laughing at the predicament we had gotten ourselves into. There we were, suddenly confined in a quiet zone where we had no escape. Who could we blame but ourselves?

In the beginning of the conversation, we earnestly tried to brainstorm ways to make our passage happier. But the fact was that the others were content, happy in their own ways. There was nothing they wanted to change. I had already exhausted all my options for change. Without Internet I couldn't ask Alexa for more ideas on "how to be happy on a crossing."

Given that we wanted the trip to be a success for the owners, I had to accept the facts as they were. This was the life the owners wanted on the boat, and it was their boat.

I tried to refocus. I was grateful for many things in life, most of them waiting for me at home. But as much as I wrinkled my forehead, squeezed my eyes, and concentrated hard on being grateful, it didn't fully result in contentment, much less being happy. Still, I told myself that I had to work harder to be content without really being content, which I was pretty sure wasn't possible. I only hoped it didn't mean I was going insane.

It took a while, but we reached a point where we were emotionally exhausted from talking about the crossing and agreed that neither of us wanted to discuss it further. We were still a team after forty years, and if nothing else worked, we'd try to find the humor in whatever happened—unless, of course, someone got hurt. Although she had never been called into action, Nurse Betty was still aboard, and she was very serious about her job.

With that topic closed, Jay began talking about a book he was reading, which caused me to yawn, turn, and move closer to him. I put my head in the crook of his shoulder, just like I did after the wet, scary trip to Key West, sighed, and promptly fell into a deep sleep. I didn't wake up until the alarm went off for our watch.

For many sailors, much of the joy of offshore sailing is found at night, while on watch. In my case, this was especially true, because I was alone with Jay at the helm in an open space that I rarely occupied during the day. My mood lifted as soon as I sat upright at the sound of the alarm, donned my life vest and tethers, and ascended the steps in the dark leading to the helm. I had only a small beam of red light from a tiny lantern that was secured to my forehead, to show the way. Between the tethers and red light and the responsibility of leading the boat through the dark night from the helm, I was like a nautical Rudolph.

I was never late for a four-hour "rotating" watch, which was the most difficult of all watch schedules, and I never slept in while Jay stayed above. Rotating sleeping patterns every night was recommended by the other couple, as they had done it once, but on our trip it meant that other crew members experienced trouble getting enough sleep. Not me, though. I always slept enough—my greatest skill.

During the watch I helped Jay bring in sails and let them out, watched for squalls, and monitored the gauges. It was a real role, and I inhabited it well. Under moonlit skies Jay and I followed the movements of large schools of dolphins playing under our navigation lights, sometimes six of them jumping all at once. On cloudy, pitch-black nights we experienced the feeling of floating in unlimited darkness, with no horizon and no city lights. We were groundless like astronauts. When an early morning squall occurred, massive rainbows crossed the horizon, their lines of color unbroken, and I took endless photographs.

Jay and I huddled together when it was cold and wet, but on bright starlit nights we would sit far apart on opposite edges of the helm sofa so we could count shooting stars. Just as we did on our most recent winter sail, I read to him from Kindle books that we both liked, and we'd talk about things we would do when we got home. It was about the future and not the past. Everything from the day before melted away.

And the end of every night watch meant we were a day closer to home.

Chapter Thirty-Four

*I*t helped that nothing really dangerous happened on our night watches other than some boats that passed too closely and a squall or two. Several nights we discovered that the autopilot gauges stopped working and needed to be rebooted. It was the worst aspect of relying on computerized gauges for everything—when they look like they're working, but they aren't.

That didn't mean there wasn't a day that scared me to my core. It occurred during one of our worst afternoon squalls, a storm with blinding rain and heavy winds, driven right at us by the trade winds. Thirty-knot straight-line winds hit us out of nowhere and Jay, as usual, ran to the foredeck to furl in the Code Zero. By the time the storm hit, the owner had totally encased all outside space in zipped up canvas and clear isinglass to prevent the rain from pummeling us. I was told to stay down below. The other couple was on watch at the helm, the husband pushing buttons and wife supposedly handling sheets.

That was the night that a lazy sheet wrapped around Jay's neck, not once, but four times.

The skies turned so dark that the owner was shining a light on my wet husband who was sitting on the slippery deck and hauling in the Code Zero against the fierce winds that were fighting to keep it open. Jay was tethered in, but tethers can't eliminate all danger. I couldn't help from below—just fruitlessly yell to the helm to secure the sheet, sounds no one could hear.

It seemed forever before Jay finished with the sail and crawled back, clamping the jack line that surrounded the boat with his double tethers, until he was safely off the foredeck of the boat.

Despite Jay's and my concerns, the lazy sheet was not locked in during the next squall as well, and once again it wrapped around Jay. That time, though, the owner was behind Jay, assisting him. I saw him as he felt it slap around his neck and he pushed it away. Once he experienced the force of the line in the wind, he understood the danger, and remedied the problem.

Many new owners worry about the wrong things, like docking, because it always seems to have an audience. The fact is that docking is not as dangerous as it is potentially embarrassing. A sailor isn't likely going to die entering a slip, especially if they are lucky enough to have twin engines and a bow thruster.

However, you can die when lines wrap around you. Sadly, early in the crossing we received notification from the ARC that emphasized that very danger—a fine French sailor on an ARC boat on the course north of us and headed straight to St. Lucia was killed when an accidental jibe occurred and his neck was wrapped by the main sheet. It was very sobering news to me, and the thought of his family's loss followed me for the remainder of the trip, and still does. It was heartbreaking.

The storm we encountered the night of the sheet incident caused a separate change at the helm. Almost immediately afterwards the other couple reacted to the squalls by making a vow not to use any sail other than a reefed self-tacking jib on their watches, not that uncommon a decision at night. They believed there was too much risk with the Code Zero.

What that really meant was that the only sail we would have while they were on watch was a few square feet of jib to move a 46-foot boat. Just like that, the slow trip became excruciatingly slower, and we fell further behind.

Many years ago I heard a motivational speaker ask the audience two questions. They were:

If someone offered you a million dollars to walk a tight rope from one high-rise building to another, would you do it? Of course not. I couldn't even look out the windows when I went to New York.

How about if they were dangling a baby on the other side? That's a different story. Of course I would.

I had two new babies dangling in front of me at the end of the trip, and one would be waiting in Grenada. The joy that led me to go on the crossing was replaced by the joy of the eventual reunion at the dock.

And that joy depended upon wind in the sails.

Just as Patrick had predicted, for the last few days the winds finally increased and blew us on a straight line toward Grenada. It was an incredible relief, but it didn't compare to the deep rumbling sound of the diesel twin engines when the owner cranked them up, which added supplemental speed. We were already more than two days behind the leaders, and the "Welcome to Grenada" parties had begun and ended.

The problem was that the delay in arrival meant that we arrived in Grenada less than twenty-four hours before Patrick, Melanie, and our new granddaughter, Greer, were expected.

The original plan was for us to spend the first couple of days of post-sailing time with the crew on the boat. That plan was made when the owner optimistically stated that the sail from Cape Verde to Grenada would last only twelve days, maybe fewer. Twelve days was a lofty goal given that the ARC suggested it would likely be fourteen, as did the stats for the average time for a catamaran of our type and size, but our crew was sure we could do it. In the end, due to lack of wind in the beginning, it took our catamaran and many others sixteen days, two more days than even the ARC predicted—also the same amount of time Columbus claimed, probably incorrectly, that he made it on his last trip.

On the upside, the Code Zero's tiny hole never enlarged and the sail operated like it was designed to do throughout the entire trip.

Arrival at the dock after any long race is almost never the "popping champagne" moment that everyone envisions, other than perhaps the first few boats over the line. It is instead rather anticlimactic. Confusion over what slip to put us in, COVID tests and dealing with customs, plus a final stressful docking all contributed to suck the joy out of the moment.

I definitely wasn't in a celebratory mood when I discovered that it was too late to make reservations for the evening's big ARC dinner.

The champagne popping was there for the owners later in the day, as if they were the owners of a horse in the Derby. Anything that happened aboard during a crossing was their sole right to claim.

Several days before we were to land, I started organizing Jay's and my belongings and packed them in their respective duffel bags. Without some preliminary packing I knew that we wouldn't be ready when it was time to leave. It helped that some of the duffel bags were filled on the flight to the Canary Islands with food and gifts for the boat: things we would leave behind, including the thankfully untouched medical kit, monitoring devices, and thick medical book, as well as the greatly used off-shore rod and reel, tackle, kitchenware, food, and a plethora of other items, big and small. In the end I had plenty of room in the bags for the return trip.

I always pack for a trip months in advance, something my friends and family at home think is funny. To me, it's a practical solution to make sure I don't forget anything when I am doing too many things at once. This time it was necessary because I believed it would take a week to gather up our belongings from all corners of the boat, and the only way to organize was to use the duffel bags to hold everything. Still, I had lots of things that needed to be done before we'd be ready to go.

First and foremost, we had a dirty sheet that I could not stand another day and a bag of dirty clothes and towels that smelled and absolutely had to be washed. The morning after arrival, I hit the marina laundry before it opened its doors. It was a good decision, because there was already a short line ahead of us. Minutes later there were boatloads of clothing in rolling carts lined up behind us.

When Jay and I approached the laundry door, the disgruntled laundress told us the clothes couldn't be ready that day, and maybe not even the next. This momentarily stunned me. All I wanted on the boat was a clean sheet and air conditioning, and if they did the laundry, I would have both of those. Clean clothes would have also been nice. Jay had been living aboard for months, and I won't even discuss the state his clothes were in.

Waiting even one day for a sheet was ridiculous, but there was no other option, since the washing machine on board was the owners to use first. Then it was the other couple, whose room it was in.

Now we had a serious dilemma.

I stood for a second or two looking at the surly woman who momentarily held the key to my happiness.

Suddenly, I couldn't think of anything other than my granddaughter who was arriving that afternoon for no purpose other than to see us. And a nice clean sheet on a hotel bed.

Jay and I are astute enough to know most of the boats had hired cleaning crews, and we were happy to contribute or even pay in full if the owner wanted to take that route. We were also happy to clean; happy to help move the boat to dry storage; happy to do most anything to button it up. And we could do it all with little effort, even if we spent the night at a hotel. I had already preliminarily cleaned our stateroom and head as a routine matter.

We were happy to do anything other than not meet my children who flew all the way to Grenada to welcome us home.

A magnet began to pull me away from the boat, and a small voice inside me told me that we weren't captives. All I had to do was leave. I had done what I promised to do and had offered to do more. They would understand.

I didn't have to stand in front of everyone in line and pull the dirty sheet out of the laundry in front of a dozen other sailors and put it back on the bed for another day and night. That humiliation could wait for another day, another person.

I left the clothes at her feet and walked away.

Before the laundress had completed checking in the next boat's load, I dialed the number for the resort where Patrick and Melanie had reservations. We reserved a room for one night—right next door to granddaughter Greer.

Jay and I reassured the owners who remained on the boat that we would return and reminded them that Patrick, also a Coast Guard captain, had volunteered to help do anything they needed, including moving the boat. We also wanted to join them for the dinners that we had paid for. I still had sailing jackets, hats, and other clothing items on the boat to retrieve. I also told the others on board that I had made sure they could come to the resort in order relax and enjoy time on the beach with us. I was leaving for Greer, not from them.

This wasn't in their plan, however, and it wasn't what they wanted. They wanted us to stay aboard and have meals with them. But I knew it was time for us to go; even if only for one day, we all needed space.

The docks were full of people like Jay and me, crew members pulling suitcases down the piers at the end of a long voyage and heading for a hotel or resort. Some were happy, but there were more unhappy sailors than I expected. I heard stories of woe from captains and a very different side from too many crew members to recount, despite crossing weather that was, in many ways, quite nice. Owners were bemoaning damage to their new boats and crew members were bemoaning the owners.

I saw a few women walking with crutches and men limping alongside them. I saw a whole lot of hangovers from uncontrolled drinking the night before. What I didn't see were a lot of smiles that early morning. It made sense; people were exhausted and the winners had already come and gone. Perhaps they had the smiles, and the smiles moved along with them.

We walked out of the marina entrance with our bags a few minutes later, still whispering to each other as we did aboard. Was it really all over?

Suddenly, there was nothing compelling enough to hold me back from who I was—a grandmother who happens to sail, not a sailor who happens to have grandchildren. I intended to enjoy being a Grenadian grandmother to the fullest.

Once we exited the marina and entered the back seat of the taxi, as I often did in the past, I put my head on Jay's shoulder and exhaled. I had kept my promise and sailed from the Canary Islands to Cape Verde, and then across the Atlantic. I'd process what it all meant later.

Now it was time to have fun in Grenada.

Chapter Thirty-Five

*I*n a few hours Greer was in my arms, a round bundle of big blue eyes with a huge smile. I FaceTimed with our son Harris and his wife Ashley and saw our other new granddaughter, Pippa, grinning and playing on her mat, and I called Jennie to catch up with Jordana, my oldest granddaughter, and her exploits. It was the best day I had in months. Jennie laughed as soon as she heard my voice, having told her brothers after she returned from the Canary Islands that she had a feeling that maybe it was going to be more difficult than I expected.

It was finally time for laughter.

While I had no expectations of Gran Canaria and Cape Verde, I did of Grenada. I'm not sure if it was the fact that it's on my side of the Atlantic or my familiarity with the people of the Caribbean. But if ever I landed in the right place at the right time, it was the Coyaba in Grenada.

The Coyaba Beach Resort was situated in the middle curve of one of the most beautiful beaches on the island. Patrick's wife Melanie chose well. The sprawling hotel looked much like it did when it was built in the eighties, with a perimeter of two stories of hotel rooms facing the water, and everything from an inviting outdoor restaurant to beach chairs and a pool bar. The rooms and restaurant were surrounded by a well-established garden designed decades ago, with hundreds of plants with flowers in vivid splashes of color. Nutmeg, cocoa, and guava trees joined the coconut trees lining walks and the edge of the beach.

I loved the sun and the shade interspersed in well-thought-out spaces to fit any preference. People were laughing and talking and playing, the sound of happy voices wafting over the waves and melding perfectly with the sounds of pleasing music from outside speakers.

Coyaba made it easy to turn one night at the hotel into a week.

For days I watched from the comfort of the beach as departing ARC boats were blown north in the strong winds offshore, headed to places like St. Lucia and further. I wondered who was on those boats and if they had a good time on the crossing. I wished them all fair winds.

Because of COVID, only a dozen of the hundred or so rooms at Coyaba were occupied. We had the first two rooms on the first floor next to the beach. Greer was the most popular guest. She slept under the palm trees (away from the coconuts) wearing a floppy hat and tiny pink sunglasses while we wiled away the days reading novels, swimming in the clear turquoise waters, and walking on the white sand beaches. We enjoyed free snorkeling over a coral reef and had use of a Hobie Cat, just in case Jay had not already sailed enough.

Slowly we became ourselves again, especially when it came to eating. I devoured a hamburger at the popular Umbrellas Beach Bar next to our hotel. Patrick and Jay bought local barbeque and I ordered local pizza—delivery, of course. Some nights we enjoyed the local dishes at the Coyaba Hotel open-air restaurant overlooking the beach. The last day we met ARC Plus friends at the Aquarium Restaurant, and after a decadent meal of seafood danced to the sounds of a local band playing the song "Sweet Caroline." The good news was that we got lots of exercise swimming and walking on the beach.

Everywhere we went the seafood was served fresh and outside with views of the harbor, the beaches, or the ocean. It was well-seasoned and cooked how I craved it after so much time away from home.

Like most tourists on Grenada, we took a private tour up the narrow winding roads through a maze of small colorful houses and shops, most constructed of concrete blocks, to the nature preserve at the top of a mountain. We visited volcanic lakes, wandered along waterfalls, ate local chocolate, and interacted with monkeys that ate from our hands and climbed on our backs. Not Greer's, of course, or mine. I threw my banana into the air the first moment that one jumped toward me.

The lack of tourism due to COVID restrictions had been tough on the islanders, but still they were as diligent about safety as anywhere I visited during COVID. We passed the tests when we arrived but were still required to show our vaccine cards to enter any establishment, and even had to sign in and leave our local address. There is a reason that Grenada had only one case of COVID before we arrived. It also makes sense that they looked warily upon the flotilla of foreigners entering their harbor, not recognizing that we sailors had already experienced the dreaded self-isolation for the last two weeks and, in our case, two days more.

We left Grenada restored and ready to tackle what waited for us after months at sea. I was ready for home.

*Never go on trips
with anyone you do not love.*

Ernest Hemingway

Part Three
Pensacola, Florida to
Isla Mujeres, Mexico

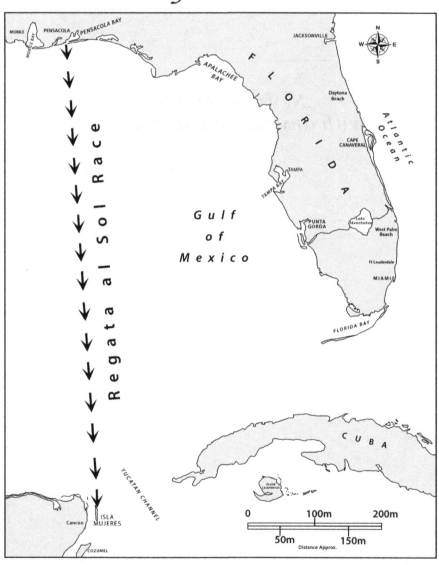

Regata al Sol Race Map

Chapter Thirty-Six

*L*ess than a month after arriving home, Jay and I sent a check to the Southern Yacht Club in New Orleans for the entry fee to the Regata al Sol: the Pensacola to Isla Mujeres, Mexico, race that is always set in May, just ahead of hurricane season. *Gypsy Lady* had a crew roster of family and friends who had sailed the race before. Two crew members would fly home and another friend would sail back on the return trip. In addition, more friends and family were flying down for the end-of-race parties.

It was the 31st race for the bi-annual event, which was conceived in 1964 by the Southern Yacht Club in New Orleans at the insistence of the Jose Lima family of Isla Mujeres, Mexico. Twenty years older than the ARC, the race changed course over the years with different starting locations, including at least one that started from Biloxi. However, for many decades the race has been co-sponsored by the Pensacola Yacht Club and the Southern Yacht Club. It begins in early May, north of Santa Rosa Island and south of the Pensacola Yacht Club.

Unlike the ARC, which is more of a rally than a race, the Regata al Sol is for serious racers, on the level of the NY to Bermuda, the LA to Hawaii, the Figawi Race from Hyannis Port to Nantucket, and other well-known offshore regional races. The biggest difference from the other regional races is that most of the boats in the Regata are in the forty-foot range, they aren't new, and the crews aren't paid, except in beer. That doesn't mean they aren't great boats, because they are—but rather that it's a smaller, hardier fleet of boats on the whole compared to boats I have seen in other races. No one intends to leave their boat for sale in Isla.

Why would Jay and I want to sail in another race so soon? It was a no-brainer—we had already upgraded the boat for the cancelled 2020 race, and had a great crew in place. Our youngest son Patrick, a captain, was going, as well as Jay's brother Bob, who is a charter fishing captain now but also retired as a Coast Guard Captain, plus two other sailing friends, Bill and David, who had completed the race many years before.

The *Gypsy Lady* crew was experienced, congenial, and ready. Better yet, they had lots of fuel and Patrick could fix any mechanical issue.

I wouldn't be Nurse Betty. There was no need to assemble another offshore medical kit like the one I left on the catamaran, thank goodness. The two friends were real medical doctors, Dr. David and Dr. Bill, as well as excellent offshore sailors.

My job was to handle logistics and communications, in addition to last-minute preparations for the race. I planned to join them in Isla Mujeres and perhaps sail on the return trip.

Over the years I've sailed and raced in the Gulf back and forth. My life was in large part molded by the Gulf and especially by its beauty, bounty, and the very real danger it represented. As a seasoned sailor who lived on the northern edge of the Gulf, I instinctively knew that this race might not be the one for me. Space was limited on the *Gypsy Lady*, the weather was forecasted to be unpredictable, and the crew was too good to cut. Given the logistics of the race into another country during COVID, I'd be a vital contribution to the team if I remained on land.

The new life vests and MOB modules would be handy in the Regata al Sol. There would be no predictable trade wind in the Gulf crossing, which might be why only two catamarans registered for 2022. Storms in the Gulf are not like the squalls we experienced in the Atlantic Ocean. In the Atlantic the squalls seldom contained lightning and seemed to consistently approach from the same direction as the trade winds blew. Gulf storms are like Zeus gone mad; for an hour he tosses lightning bolts at your feet from every direction for absolutely no reason at all beyond his bad mood, and tops it off with gale force gusts.

Gulf waves aren't like swells in the Atlantic, with sometimes more than fifty meters between the crests—they're more like concrete retaining walls with barely a few feet separating one from the next.

Even worse, late cold fronts from the north or west can cause some tricky conditions, which is probably why the insurer wanted verification that we had installed navigation maps of Cuba and Honduras.

The thought of an early tropical storm was troublesome.

Periods of calm were almost as bad—long, hot, humid, and miserable.

It sounded like fun.

The Gulf of Mexico is shaped like a bladder with two holes on the bottom for water ingress and egress—one hole is off the tip of the Yucatan near the coast of Isla, and the other hole is between Cuba and Key West (Florida Straits). One of the most significant and powerful currents in the world is contained within it: the Gulf Loop. The Gulf Loop is between 125 and 190 miles wide and flows at about 2.5 knots through the heart of the Gulf before exiting in the Florida Straits and finally heading north up the east coast of Florida as a vital part of the Gulf Stream.

The Regata al Sol and Regata del Sol, the latter of which starts in St. Petersburg, are the only United States offshore races that require sailors to navigate in and around the powerful Loop current.

Benjamin Franklin, who called the Gulf Stream current "a river in the ocean" and spent a lifetime studying it, drew maps that showed the Loop's warm waters as they merged into the Florida Straits. Ernest Hemingway's books pulse with the ebb and flow of the rich beginnings of the Gulf Stream that mark the end of the Loop. Today we don't need the literary imagery to describe the Loop – we have radar. On radar we see the Loop as a thick, deep red ligament, coursing its way around the Gulf like a python.

Biloxi, as well as most of the upper Gulf Coast, experiences the very rare diurnal tide, as in only one high and one low tide in a day. That phenomenon is caused by the power of the Gulf Loop which doesn't allow the Gulf water to ebb and flow with the moon's gravitational pull as easily as it does almost everywhere else on the planet. It's that forceful.

The Loop also has another significant environmental impact. Although the lack of upper-level steering winds and the presence of moisture in the atmosphere are two main factors in the creation and direction of a hurricane, the warmth of the Gulf waters and the eddies created by the Loop's outside edges also contribute to the energy of a hurricane.

Cape Verde's waters may spawn hurricanes, but I see the Gulf Loop as a hurricane's day care provider, supplying the formula and environmental conditions favorable for storms to intensify before making landfall.

Luckily the Regata has always been scheduled earlier than the beginning of hurricane season. In May the Loop is more like a racetrack that can both contribute to speed or inhibit it, depending on the heading of a sailboat.

As the 2022 race began, satellite images displayed a bright reddish-orange color indicating a strong Loop current moving north from Isla along a rhumb line to New Orleans. If *Gypsy Lady* was caught in this northward current it would cut her speed in half, given the light winds forecasted for the first half of the race. Catching the southerly flow of the loop current was vital to sailors in the race. To do so meant they would have to stay well east or west of the rhumb line.

However, sailing a current isn't the same as driving down the right-hand lane of a road. It's more like trying to follow a drunk driver at night from a distance. While the current may show up on maps in bright red and then fade to yellow as it exits the Gulf, the ever-moving Loop is largely invisible to the boater above it.

Despite having no brightly marked line to follow or set of markers indicating the current's direction or borders, a good sailor knows whether he or she is in the current. In past centuries a boat's performance was an indication of current direction and strength. Observant sailors would judge their location by the surface of the water—they would calculate the wind speed and direction and see if waves were flattening or stacking up with short periods between crests. Even the pattern or diagonal array of Sargassum weed that floats near the water's surface was instructive.

With all the electronic advantages of today, sailors can easily discern whether the current is with or against them and how much the current is affecting their boat speed. GPS informs racers of their speed over ground, which they compare to their speed through the water, as indicated by a small paddle wheel mounted deep under the hull. It isn't too difficult to calculate on a minute-by-minute basis the impact of the Loop current.

Not even the best sailor can rely on the Loop to always help move the boat along, however. Even if our boat negotiated the Loop perfectly, eventually, when *Gypsy Lady* sailed close to Isla, the current would be against her. If unlucky and the wind was too light or from the wrong direction, she'd have difficulty crossing the current without being driven northward away from Isla. The risks were daunting.

I had all the faith in the world that the crew could handle almost anything Mother Nature threw their way, and sea-kindly *Gypsy Lady* was chomping at the bit to race.

My job was to be their guardian on shore.

Chapter Thirty-Seven

*I*n late April our twelve-year-old grand-daughter Jordana helped Jay and me move *Gypsy Lady* from Biloxi to Pensacola during her spring break, like her mother often did as a child, continuing the circle of life. The weather was typically awful that time of the year—the winds were twenty-five knots from the north and east, and vicious currents fought against us the entire way. It made Jordana's inaugural crossing across Mobile and Pensacola Bay with her grandparents "epic," as she described it.

The upside, she said, was that when it was over, we opted to stay at Lulu's two nights instead of one, giving her lots of time to play with friends that she met there.

The truth is that no one, not one single person I ever met, has referred to crossing Mobile Bay in loving terms. It is lovely to see from a white wooden bench on a Fairhope dock while sipping a mint julep, but once a person toys with the idea of entering the water by boat, the bay's dark underbelly exposes itself like a rising sea monster. Pensacola Bay, with its deep ship's channel funneling between islands, was not much better.

Finishing the trip across the two bays, as bad as it was, had upsides other than Lulu's. For us it meant that the boat was safely in Pensacola in plenty of time for final preparations.

I provisioned the boat for the week to Isla and the return sail home, with the input of the crew. It was easy and fun. Dr. Bill wanted to make his specialty, red beans and rice, and said he would bring everything for two meals. He also brought both coffee and peanuts that he roasted. Patrick packed steaks and marinated sausages in his Yeti cooler for grilling. I slow-cooked a large pork loin for pulled pork sandwiches. Bob brought candied salmon from Alaska. Dr. David and I shopped for staples, breads, milks, fruit, and lots of snacks, plus bio-degradable plates. Another Bill, who would be replacing Dr. Bill on the return trip, bought everything needed for first class sushi.

I labeled all the cabinets with yellow post-it notes identifying the contents within them, so hungry men could locate food without effort. I didn't want anyone forced to search for sustenance, especially in rough seas. They only needed one laminated map—the one for fire extinguishers and safety equipment.

For me, the hardest part of the preparation was the completion of the endless notarized paperwork to get the crew and boat through customs to Mexico and then back home. If there was any reason I felt that one of us needed to be on dry land, it was to make sure this process went smoothly.

It was only when the paperwork for the trip was completed, the race started, and the boat was under sail, that I was ready to fly to Mexico.

The Regata al Sol was orchestrated—from operations room to rum parties—at the funky hotel Cabanas del mar Maria on the stunning North Beach of Isla Mujeres.

Isla Mujeres is an island about six miles long, twenty-five minutes by ferry across the bay from Cancun, 550 miles due south of my home as the crow flies, and less than 150 miles from Cuba.

Jennie, Melanie, baby Greer, Mel's mom Michalle, and I flew to Cancun by plane on a Saturday with almost fifty other Regata family members, friends, and past participants who wouldn't dare miss the parties. Do I need to tell anyone what it was like with about forty of us on one plane? On another plane there were many more, plus an eight-month-old baby, stroller, car seat, and diaper bag with six bottles of baby water and cans of formula, all of which had to be individually checked with testing strips by security?

Once in Cancun we navigated a confusing mass of people outside the terminal to find our shuttle to the ferry, which dropped us off at the ferry dock where we merged into yet another mass of confused people. This time we were bogged down in a ferry ticket misunderstanding—a lost-in-translation moment. It was only after we exited the ferry, exhausted and already showing a bit of sunburn, that we arrived in the tiny, busy downtown of Isla Mujeres.

Because of Mel's mom's sprint down the ferry dock and awe-inspiring leap onto a moving ferry, all of the family and luggage, together with Greer, Mel, and Jennie, arrived intact. The hotel staff saw our bedraggled crew and wisely put us in neighboring hotel rooms in a small three-story tower over the operations room.

When the Regata began its first race, the ferry to the island was not so busy and the island was quainter. Then, just as it was becoming a favored tourist destination, COVID stopped the influx of tourists for a year or more, destroying the fragile economy. In May of 2022, it was back with a bang. Isla exploded with day-trippers from Cancun, seasoned international tourists, and Americans buying homes.

Even with this new growth, Isla Mujeres is still an island without cars other than taxis, where everyone rides in gas-powered golf carts or motorbikes, no safety equipment added, and where American restaurant chains or franchises have yet to arrive.

Once in Isla, I couldn't help but compare the four very different and exotic islands I had visited in less than six months: Gran Canaria, Cape Verde, and Grenada, and finally Isla Mujeres. Gran Canaria was sleek and modern, quintessentially Spanish; Cape Verde, traditional African; Grenada, Caribbean to the core. Isla Mujeres is authentically Mexican, and in all the best ways, with its lively music, street vendors, colorful buildings, and brightly embroidered clothes.

It turned out that the island closest to home was the one that tugged at my heart the strongest. Although battered by recent hurricanes and its economy still recovering from COVID, the smiling, happy entrepreneurs that lined the streets of Isla with their small shops and food trucks, and even the professional guides hawking tours that met us at the ferry, were unfailingly optimistic about the future and warmly welcomed us.

The Cabanas del mar Maria wasn't the Coyaba in Grenada, but it was definitely the most inviting, warm, and quirky hotel I've ever visited. Between the views, the beach bar, the people, the sunsets, the light turquoise waters, and sandy beach, it was my version of five-star.

All of the Regata parties—and there were parties every day for a week—were held under the massive thatched roof that towered over our hotel's beach bar. The roof was supported on its corners and sides with roughly hewn beams, atop of which sat four enormous walls of tightly wrapped thatch, soaring upwards to form a point at least fifty feet high. It was the ultimate tiki hut.

Tables and long buffets were set in the sand underneath, covered in white cloths with red woven runners, and always ready for the evening's menu of ceviche, guacamole, and other local dishes. A small band occupied a riser on the edge of the bar away from the tables. The singer was there almost all day, her melodious voice offering up pleasing songs to our balconies as we sat and held Greer in the late afternoons, watching the sunset.

Only the bar, which served endless rum drinks and margaritas, had a tiled floor. Shoes were always optional.

Like most of our last two years, the restaurants we visited outside of the hotel were also open-air, with shade from pergolas and local trees and masses of cascading pink bougainvillea. Once in the shade we were further cooled by the afternoon trade winds. We dined on everything from street tacos and grilled corn to salads covered with fruit, bowls of guacamole, and chocolate churros.

The best part of the Regata was that it had a large core of friends and family who had been sailing in it for years and knew all the ropes. At first I found it hard to figure out the complex operations of the race and the more nuanced, but highly tuned social scene. To know me is to know that this would frustrate me until I cracked the code.

It wasn't like things weren't out in the open to see, which was the opposite of the corporate atmosphere of the ARC where all operations were roped off and entry by participants prohibited. I felt insignificant even among the least important of the ARC officials. In the Regata it was totally different: transparent and open, and everyone was willing to help. But you had to know what you were looking for in order to get the right response, and I knew absolutely nothing.

While I was sipping mojitos by the pool and probing people for information about parties, *Gypsy Lady* was experiencing her own learning curve: sailing with almost no wind. This felt especially unfair and ironic after a month of monstrous, often gale-force, winds that had already worked to trim the number of Regata participants.

Where did the winds go?

Chapter Thirty-Eight

G ypsy Lady was not a light wind kind of girl. She doesn't like to point (after all, she's not a dog) and, just so you know, she also doesn't like to back up.

Jay started the race with a light wind sail we had just purchased, but the sail, which we don't usually use, was not up to the task. It quickly needed a small repair, something the crew members handled as a routine matter, having done it many times before, but it isn't the type of sail we care to carry on board at home or use a lot. The crew wasn't disappointed when Jay changed to a more trustworthy sail. Another boat had the same issue with its new light wind sail, but attempted no repairs. They simply pulled it down and replaced it with their old one.

Once I heard that information, and given the crossing experience, I decided that light wind sails are like light weight boyfriends. Who knows if they will hang around. And they are very needy.

On Gypsy Lady the sail was replaced by our large genoa that moved the boat faster on its easterly track to catch the Loop on its southerly journey. Jay had some catching up to do due to the sail switch. But that was soon to change.

While I was still making connections on shore and not yet in the know on everything, about 200 miles out from Pensacola Gypsy Lady and a handful of other boats ran into a bank of vicious storms that formed in their path, battering them with large waves and rain. News was out that one boat was demasted and the crew had to be rescued by the Coast Guard. Friends and family in Florida sent me the articles so I could get details. The men on Gypsy Lady had more to do than call me on the satellite phone, and I didn't call them.

Another boat also had mast and rigging issues but sailed on its own accord to the nearest port, which was Tampa. A third boat, a multihull, returned to the Gulf Coast, but I didn't know why.

All I could tell from Kattack, the Regata monitoring website, was that *Gypsy Lady* was plugging ahead, crew most likely drenched and cabin probably in disarray, not knowing the fate of their fellow boats.

When I received word of the demasting, I was upset for the crew but also glad Jay made a last-minute decision in Pensacola to replace all the stays on the boat and have our rigging re-inspected. They might still have trouble, but it was one less thing to worry about.

After the storm, I continued to follow Jay on Kattack, constantly checking the screen like a social media addict. On Kattack the entries were depicted as tiny little boats on the screen—ours was red. And our little red boat was not doing so well.

Many of the boats had taken the westerly tack toward Texas and then intended to cross the Gulf Stream when closer to Isla. That group was ahead. The small group that remained with Jay on the east side was lagging behind. But that was only for a short while; halfway to Isla a problem arose that affected all the boats.

The wind completely died. The computer screen suddenly showed tiny boats scattered in the middle of the Gulf like brightly colored toys in a child's bathtub, drifting and pointing in all kinds of directions, none of them toward Isla. 0.6, 0.8, 1.6…no one was moving. For hours and hours they baked in the brutally hot sun, going nowhere.

I wasn't the only one watching the boat's movements. Our son Harrison was monitoring the winds and currents and weather predictions minute by minute back in New Orleans. He was a great sailor himself, and but for work would have been aboard. The only problem was that he was too much like his dad.

I'd call him when I was worried. The conversations went something like this:

"It looks like there might be wind in an hour or two," I'd say, my voice light and happy like a TV weather forecaster, as if that made my information more reliable.

"Mom, you're delusional."

At which point I would tell him he was like his father, and we'd banter like that until he really did have to focus on work instead of watching *Gypsy Lady*.

But I didn't give up. I would call every four or five hours to see what he thought, frustrated that our boat was barely moving and seeking some reassurance. Finally, he started answering the phone with "Hot Line for False Hope."

I stopped trying to convince him things were going better than they were.

That realization made it even more shocking to me when I saw the boats on the westerly tack begin to move, and to move much faster. How could it be? Where did the wind come from? It didn't appear on Windy. com predictions. It looked to me like they were using their engines, but surely not. These were some of the best boats in the race.

By then, I had familiarized myself with the Regata operations and made friends. I was comfortable enough to drop in the operations center to see as, one by one, skippers reported to the race committee that they had, indeed, turned their "engine on"—they were out of the race. Unlike the ARC, which permitted engine use for a significant percentage of the crossing, the Regata al Sol was a real race and forbade engine use in any circumstance other than to rescue another boat.

These were not fair-weather sailors, but they knew where they would stand if they stayed the course. They knew the odds against them when crossing into the northerly flow of the Loop current with no wind from the west. Some crews on one or two boats weren't prepared for a race of six days or more. They had obligations. One had a sick crew member. Many had won the race before. It wasn't a "do or die" race, and there was no dishonor in heading to the beach and the parties.

All of a sudden, the once overwhelming competition was dwindling.

Quietly and steadily *Gypsy Lady* sailed southeasterly until I thought she was going to Cuba, and only then did the wind finally fill in behind her from the east and the spinnaker came out. One tack and she had a straight reach into Isla. It took five days to get the right wind and direction but finally she was in her element, making a strong finish.

Each day until that moment, as I waited in and outside of the operations room, I was repeatedly asked if Jay would turn on the engine.

"Never," I said as I watched the tiny red boat on the large computer screen. I felt like I was playing a part in Braveheart, almost beating my chest with a fist in defiance.

Patrick notified me at about midnight on Tuesday that *Gypsy Lady* would arrive at two in the morning. I went to the operations office, where two race committee members were patiently waiting.

That news triggered a full alert in the office in order to monitor the boat's position and movements so that the race officials could contact the escort boat and the Isla customs authorities when *Gypsy Lady* was closing in on the finish line. The problem was that on that particular night at 2:00 a.m. the person monitoring on the Mexican end of the calls spoke no English. It was a frustrating situation. No matter what was said, the response was ambiguous enough to us to be concerned that no one was on their way to escort Jay.

The race officials were getting exasperated as I sat there trying to figure out the role of Echo, a Mexican naval ship anchored at the finish line, and Juliet, the smaller vessel that would escort *Gypsy Lady* to her berth.

"You're going to have to go upstairs and get your daughter," I was eventually directed by the head of the committee. "We need her."

"Jennie," I said a few seconds later, tapping on her door just hard enough to get her attention, "the race officials have asked if you could come down and help."

Dressed only in her short, flowered silk nightgown, without a word she stepped out and shut the door behind her, and then ran down the slippery tile staircase steps coated in sand, into the operations room. She didn't ask why—fluent in Spanish, she had been translating for everyone in our group for days.

Once there, she was quickly instructed on the use of the VHF and proceeded to translate the questions and answers for the officials, ensuring that her father, brother, and uncle would be safely escorted through the temporary channel markings. Time was of the essence, as they were already negotiating an unfamiliar and challenging finishing corridor, with an out-cropping of coral that could not be seen at night and a lot of wind and current. I also knew they were exhausted.

In less than five minutes we had definitive answers that the escort boat was on its way. A few minutes later the officials and I walked out to the beach and saw *Gypsy Lady*'s mast, her blue spreader lights, and the red lights of the escort coming around the island, a beautiful sight against the dark waters and pitch-black night sky. They had rounded the final mark.

An hour later the race officials, customs officers and I cheered *Gypsy Lady*'s finish as the crew threw the lines to us in the Isla Mujeres Yacht Club Marina. I was relieved to see Jay arrive, and even happier when, despite the early morning hours, the crew completed paperwork in record time at a table set up by customs and immigration at the end of the dock. The last hurdle was for Patrick to back *Gypsy Lady* into a slip against howling wind and wicked current that wanted to push her bow to the beach. He was able to corral her in like a recalcitrant horse, without a scratch. But once again, she made it clear: she doesn't like to back up.

Chapter Thirty-Nine

A round my neck were three old-fashioned keys on yellow strings for David, Bill, and Bob's hotel rooms, which Jennie and I had readied for their arrival, especially careful to turn on the air conditioning and leave ice-cold bottles of waters. Despite the beautiful boats in the race and power on the dock, a great marina bar and grill, and a nice beach, I knew that the sailors would hit the hotels as soon as they passed customs. Vacation world was onshore.

The boats' needs could wait until the rum cocktails, margaritas, and warm beach sand had done their magic.

Gypsy Lady was last to arrive, which meant that the race committee could also begin the process of tallying final times adjusted with handicaps. The fact that she was last to arrive is a testament to the accuracy of the handicap system, which had calculated that *Gypsy Lady* should be the slowest boat to finish the race. Handicaps attempt to equalize the boats and make it all about the sailors.

The next morning Jay and I attended a reception at the Rock House, an old limestone and coral stone house owned by the descendants of Jose de Lima, the champion of tourism in Isla Mujeres and mastermind behind the initial Regata al Sol. The house is built on a jagged outcropping of rocks on the northwest side of the island with windows situated for stunning views. Turquoise water swirled through open spaces in the surrounding rocks, all carved over time by incoming tides. The house melded perfectly into its setting, so much so that we thought from a distance that it was just a clump of rocks. Up close it was architecturally perfect.

Mr. Lima died in 2009 at the age of 97, and since then the house has been used primarily to host the regattas that he loved. It's more akin to a historical museum than a home, with almost every inch of wall space covered in old pictures, past Regata al Sol posters, and memorabilia such as Jacques Cousteau's camera. Mr. Cousteau once lived six months in the house and filmed there on two occasions.

Cognizant of the dangers of incoming storms, when one is approaching the family removes all the household's contents—rooms full of items, furnishings, and paintings—and later returns each one to the exact same place they were located before the storm.

Time seemed to stand still while I wandered the house, drink in hand, breezes blowing through the open windows and doors—a home well loved by a person who, even after death, is still revered by the community and Regata al Sol sailors of today and the past.

It was the first time that Jay and I could sense the deep level of respect and friendship that the Regata and Isla officials had developed over their sixty-year relationship. The speeches that were given, the presence of the distinguished admiral, the current mayor's representative, and other dignitaries, plus members of the Lima family, reaffirmed everything we were told by the Southern Yacht Club officials.

After Mr. Lima's death, his family wanted to contribute to the Regata in his name. They presented the Southern Yacht Club with a large ornate Mexican silver trophy, molded in the shape of an urn with curved handles. It proudly displays a replica of the Southern Yacht Club flag on one of its smooth sides and on the other, in elaborate script, details the award for sportsmanship in sailing it is meant to represent. The honor is intended to be given by the Regata al Sol race committee to sailors who behave in such a way as to make the Regata proud—sailors who help others, who show kindness and professionalism.

It took a lot of speeches, stories, and a thorough tour of his house before I understood it wasn't just the Regata or the tiny Isla Mujeres Yacht Club—Mr. Lima was important to sailing in general. Jose de Lima spent his whole life working to ensure that sailboat races, as well as tourism, continued to exist on his island, even in those dark days after the Cuban missile crises. His story—the hard work, obstacles overcome, and sacrifices that he made for the good of his beloved island, and his focus on offshore racing, of course—is deeply touching. It was a good life that other sailors would do well to emulate.

The next day Jay, Patrick, Michalle, Jennie, and I went on a snorkeling trip in a government-protected zone off the island—not exactly a

Jacques Cousteau experience, but so much fun. I'm not usually a happy snorkeler, as I have poor eyesight underwater, but this wasn't the case in Isla. The water was crystal clear and yielded a panorama of different species of colorful and exotic fish up close, with a large barracuda or two in the mix.

By three in the afternoon, we had visited three sites, including statues, and were exhausted, especially from those times when we fought the current. The heat of the day and hours of snorkeling had taken their toll. We took off our masks and prepared to return to the hotel and shower, only to be told instead that it was time to eat.

Eat?

Amazingly, the trip included an afternoon meal prepared by our snorkeling guide. We were too intrigued to complain about the time.

The guide and his assistant took us by boat to a beach with a large, open-air concrete building on one end. It most resembled an old fish market. We sat at a long concrete table, and on a smaller table the two guides carefully deboned fresh grilled fish and artfully served it to us on biodegradable plates with rice, tortillas, and salsa. It was the best fish I had eaten in months. Our guide, Captain Barboni, was not only informative, but he was very environmentally conscious, to the extent that he forbade anyone aboard to apply sunblock because of the damage it can cause to the coral reefs.

By the time we were finished eating, all the long tables in the building had filled with happy Mexican families resting or eating after a long day, along a few surprised and confused tourists like us. It was a bustling, happy place, one that we ordinarily would have no desire to leave—but there was more on our schedule.

We needed to return to the hotel for the traditional golf cart Mardi Gras parade that the Regata families and sailors put on for the local children of the island. As instructed, we retrieved the large bags of beads and toys that I had temporarily stored in the anchor locker of the boat in order to throw them from our golf cart, which was to be decorated like a float.

At five in the evening, at least forty carts with balloons and streamers were escorted by the police through the town while the children and some adults, all who seemed to know the drill, stood patiently waiting with small bags along the route to catch them. No one in our cart had ever thrown beads and toys, and it showed, but, like the snorkeling, it was an unanticipated amount of fun.

It was a long day and, after a dinner with the crew, we ended the evening early. The biggest and last event was scheduled for the next evening—the Trophy dinner and party.

Chapter Forty

*T*he Trophy Party was the first time that I saw all of the boat crews together. I was stunned by how many people we knew that arrived on other boats. Melanie reconnected with a high school friend, and Patrick discovered that he knew her brother. I saw a distant cousin we had raced against for thirty years, and who once again beat us across the finish line. My best friend's brother-in-law and his wife, who stayed in our house after Katrina, were also there.

By then the *Gypsy Lady* crew was part of the group, new and old, melding into a boisterous montage of friends and family, like children who go to camp and after only a week cry because they don't want to ever leave their new best friends.

There had been several parties over the course of the week, all with margaritas and food, but I knew the Trophy party was different from the moment I saw the sandy-floored room transformed with elaborate decorations hanging from its cross beams. Everything was more over-the-top than the weekly parties—from food to wait service to displays to dignitaries. Even the wall-sized Regata al Sol race board had been covered in large flags from Mexico, the U.S., and participating Yacht Clubs.

In front of the race board were cloth-covered tables lined with shiny silver trophies, including a trophy with a carved boat on it, as well as another large circular trophy, more of a work of art, to be presented. Other tables held the buffet lines of food and desserts.

Guy, the emcee, and an accompanying music player, stood at a podium with a microphone, along with two women who presented the trophies. The men helped to pump up the large crowd that had assembled for the evening, every table full. Guy was sometimes campy, but always witty and a whole lot of fun. The crowd pulsated with the music and cheered on the sailors as they walked up for their trophies.

We could enjoy it all. Jay and I had no stress. It was our boat, and we didn't care who won. The most likely winners were our friends, and we wished them well. At best, we figured we would place third in the cruising spinnaker class B, and that would be amazing enough.

Perhaps that mindset is why Jay was in such a state of shock when he was called to the stage and awarded the Jose de Lima Sportsmanship trophy, the large Mexican silver urn with a smooth swirling surface and large curved handles, sitting high on a pedestal.

I always knew that Jay was a great sport, but I wondered how the committee had decided it as well. He was absolutely floored and deeply appreciative.

We couldn't keep the trophy and haul it around Biloxi, which was probably a very wise decision by the race committee. We were contented to wait for one day to take lots of photographs of it in its permanent location at the Southern Yacht Club in the club's impressive trophy case, and to keep the large silver platter that memorialized the honor.

As we all know in sailing, the last can be first and the first can be last, and due to handicapping sometimes a sailboat can be both last and first together. In the 2022 Regata we weren't first, and the first wasn't last, but with adjusted times *Gypsy Lady* ended up with a respectable third place overall in the cruising class. The winners ahead of us sailed spectacularly well under the conditions. Equally good sailing and perseverance paid off for the crew of *Gypsy Lady*.

Gypsy Lady's crew received two third-place platters and, my favorite, a beautiful Mexican pewter tray embossed with raised images of sea life around the edges, which we received for being the "Turtle." As I told the committee repeatedly, *Gypsy Lady* wasn't last—the crew didn't turn on her engines—but I also wanted to keep the tray.

In fact, I have always gravitated to being called the tortoise rather than the hare. Maybe the award was a sign of something.

As the evening wound down, I sat at the table, moonlight shining off the water. My eyes surveyed the room around me—tables full of tired but happy people with a common love of sailing, all but the babies engaged in animated conversations.

Sailing the Regata was an accomplishment. The sailors and their families and friends had a right to celebrate.

I turned my attention to the smiling faces around my own table, their hot and slightly sunburnt cheeks all glistening under the soft lights strung from the Tiki roof rafters.

Even though they're all adults now, Jay's and my children fell into their familiar roles seamlessly. From Patrick's navigation and detailed preparation of the boat, to Harris and Jennie's onshore support, it was a happy family affair. Their enthusiasm was infectious.

The wild thing about the Regata is that Jay and I weren't trophy seekers. In our amateur status, we traveled over five thousand miles on a sailboat in 2021, and if we add all of the miles we've sailed over forty years it's been tens of thousands. It all began because of friends at school and endured because of our marriage and the betterment of our family. It was never for the accolades.

We raced for fun, and there was nothing like good-natured racing to build the children's skills through team building. For the boys, Wednesday night races that cost nothing had all the intensity and rivalry of a Rolex offshore. They didn't want syndicates looking for big money advertisers, just ordinary competitors vying for bragging rights.

Our children learned hands-on the geometry, mathematics, meteorology, engine mechanics, navigation, and sportsmanship of sailing, on their own time, over many years. They didn't have to live on a boat. It was okay to have a permanent home.

Chapter Forty-One

*I*sla was our home for a week, but all great things must eventually come to an end, or they become perceptibly less great with each passing hour. Jennie couldn't understand why we didn't leave the boat in Isla for a month. President Biden had slackened restrictions on Cuba, and Jay and I had always wanted to sail there, forbidden for so long. After all these years, it was so close.

But it was too late and there were too many moving parts to postpone our trip home. The children had things to do, places to be, and lives to live. The warm Loop current flowing north would wait for no man, especially us.

On the last morning of our stay I walked barefoot with Jennie from our room and then along the white sands of North Beach, knowing that in a matter of hours my freedom from shoes would end. A few minutes earlier the beach vendors had finished their sunrise ritual of "sweeping" the sand into neat tiny lines, all of which would quickly disappear under a mass of footsteps beginning with us. It was so much effort for such a fleeting moment of perfection.

We were both lost in thought when we made the turn back to our hotel, my mind primarily focused on the trip home.

It was Jennie who broke the silence.

"You know, you're always going to be mostly known for crossing the Atlantic on a sailboat."

"I hope not," I said, stopping to look at her.

She gave me a rueful smile. She'd noticed that I had avoided talking about the crossing for most of the Regatta, and when anyone brought it up, I diverted the topic.

"Yeah. Even the people in my office think it is cool that you sailed across the Atlantic Ocean."

People I didn't even know were genuinely interested?

I was surprised. Of all the meaningful things in life I had seen and done, I never considered the ARC in the running of the top ten. It wasn't because of the lack of fun. I had suffered much more unhappiness in my lifetime. Certainly, I had endured more physical challenges and worry. And definitely I had experienced more joy.

I turned and looked across the calm bay toward the high-rise condominiums in Cancun. How had this occurred? Was an ocean crossing what I wanted the world to remember about me—my legacy?

Maybe if I was a professional sailor or had given my life to the sport as so many do—or perhaps if I was an amazing technical writer—I would have talked more about the crossing. But I knew I was a recreational sailor. In my mind I was still Patti Jane, not a conquering hero. I didn't deserve any glory. That was reserved for the solo sailors and the record breakers.

As I stood there pondering, Jennie walked away from me to find shade as the sun began to bear down upon us. Only then did I sigh and roll my head around to work out an early morning crick, then look up at the few remaining pink morning clouds wafting above us. She was right. It was undeniable.

After all those incredibly busy months since Grenada—when I had no time for any ruminations—it finally sunk in.

I crossed the Atlantic on a sailboat. I really did it.

Very few ever do.

I carefully prepared for months, overcame my fears, sailed in winds over thirty knots and waves twelve feet tall, held tight in vicious squalls that came up one after the other in rows behind us, endured the boredom, and survived the rest, all while my husband Jay remained beside me. Others who started the venture were not so fortunate. And I had been to Cape Verde, an almost mythical destination, not to mention the Canary Islands and Grenada.

Prior to COVID, I couldn't have imagined the amazing events that would occur in 2021. They were definitely not lifelong goals of mine. But adventures did unfold like pages in a book, because of good luck, good health, and perseverance. I'm sure there were other unknown forces at play. All I know is that I experienced life in a way that few people get the opportunity to do. So, to do anything other than embrace each experience would be ungrateful.

I had to face the facts. Even after I completed the crossing, I'm still impressed by those who also did it—some with worse circumstances and others better. I know the demons many battled inside and out when times were tough.

Life is funny. The passage of time has a way of compressing the bad memories and increasing the recall of the good. This feels especially true for sailors. Forty-nine days to be challenged, mostly at sea, isn't very long in a well-lived life.

At the end of any race, whether metaphorical or actual, it's the result that matters. Did you finish the race or quit when the going got tough.

I finished.

I turned my back to the water and walked toward Jennie, who waited for me on a wooden swing near the hotel beach bar.

"You're right—now that I have time to think about it, I have to admit I never thought I would do it, but…"

She stood and cocked her head and looked at me, ready to groan if the topic was to continue.

"But," I started again, "are you telling me it will be on my tombstone? Not that I will…"

She laughed and turned to walk to the hotel doors before I could go further.

I guess that meant yes.

I found it interesting that Jennie didn't bother to ask me the one question interviewers always ask of sailors who crossed an ocean. It's the inquiry reporters also ask mountain climbers, marathoners, and swimmers who cross the channel even before they have showered off.

Would they do it again?

Or, in my case, would I?

My gut answer is no, or at least not the same way. But the truth is that I'll never know until I leave this life, all the hatches tightened down, sails permanently covered. "Maybe" is the best answer. Maybe one day I'll be shocked to find myself crossing the Pacific, but like the Atlantic, it's not on my bucket list, and there are many other choices in the way.

Whether I do or not, I'm confident there is no need for me to prove anything, even to myself. I'm happy in my life as a coastal sailor on *Gypsy Lady*. I continue to make treasured memories on the waters nearest my home, and I don't have to leave family for months, maybe years, to enjoy life. I'll still travel and sail to new places—but reaching to grow, not to escape where I'm from.

Just like it was for Ulysses in his adventure, I discovered long ago that home is the ultimate destination.

Acknowledgments

*O*ver the last forty years so many people have influenced the direction of my life that it is impossible to name them all. But for the crazy captain in Key West forty years ago, Jay and I would not be a couple. But for the failed COVID test of Craig and Jill we wouldn't have left the house in January. Every dockmaster and friendly harbor in storms, all the people we met along the way, and especially the family and friends over the years who invited us out on their boats and, better yet, the ones who sailed with us on our boats—I give each one of you my humblest thanks. You all helped create who I am today.

I also want to thank those who helped to create this book and volunteered to read it, especially Karen and Matt, who are always there with their sage words of wisdom.

Finally, I am a grateful for the men in my life: my father, brothers, husband, sons, and cousins. As the only girl in the mix for most of my life, they surrounded me with encouragement, free shuttles, and more than a little bit of candid, but nonetheless, loving advice.

And thank you Jennie, Harris, and Patrick for always making me laugh at myself.

Thanks are also due to Amber Kait Photography and Julia Nelson Photography.

About the Author

*J*ane Golden is an avid sailor and lifelong boating enthusiast. She is also a hopeless romantic when it comes to sailing and sailors. In fact, she met her husband sailing from Destin, Florida, to Key West and raised two sons and a daughter, all of whom are excellent sailors in their own right.

As a serial sailboat owner, racer, cruiser, and unpaid crew member on friends' boats, she accumulated a wealth of knowledge to convey to women who wish to sail but find it a daunting task given their busy lives. She knows there is no requirement to leave everything and everyone behind, and circumnavigate the globe in order to discover the joy of sailing. Whether on a trip near-shore or far, small vessel or large, all sailors get the same rush of adrenaline when they gather the confidence to drop the dock-lines.

45408113R00109